D0119713

THE DILEMMA
OF DEMOCRACY

THE DILEMMA
OF DEMOCRACY

Diagnosis and Prescription

LORD HAILSHAM

COLLINS
St James's Place, London
1978

William Collins Sons & Co Ltd
London · Glasgow · Sydney · Auckland
Toronto · Johannesburg

First published April 1978
Reprinted May 1978

ISBN 0 00 211860 2

Set in Baskerville
Made and Printed in Great Britain by
William Collins Sons & Co Ltd Glasgow

To My Wife

And Elijah came unto all the people and said:
'How long halt ye between two opinions? If the
Lord be God, follow him, but if Baal, then follow him.'
And the people answered him not a word.

I Kings XVIII 21

CONTENTS

TWO KINDS
OF DEMOCRACY

The genesis of this book lay in a desire to rethink my own political philosophy. I had often been urged to write a third edition of my *Case for Conservatism*, but, from the first, I saw that this was impossible. It was not that I regretted what I had said in that book, or that I thought it incapable of improvement. It was that I no longer believed that a simple defence of my own party or its philosophy matched the need of the time.

The difficulty was that at first I hardly knew how to formulate what I wished to say. In part I wished to establish a political philosophy. In part I wished to produce a programme of constitutional and political change.

As I wrote, it gradually became clear to me what was in my mind. Our troubles derive from the fact that we are halting between two inconsistent opinions about the nature of democracy, indeed about the nature and function of government, and between the two we are unable to make up our minds. Both opinions claim to be democratic. Both assert they are libertarian. Both claim to rest upon the interest of the people. Yet each is wholly inconsistent with the other. The politics of the next twenty-five years may well depend upon the encounter between the two, and more will depend on the outcome than the future of the British Islands. The two theories are the theory of centralized democracy, known to me as elective dictatorship, and the theory of limited government, in my language the doctrine of freedom under law.

Between the two theories there can ultimately be no compromise. Both may depend upon universal adult suffrage. But the one will assert the right of a bare majority in a single chamber assembly, possibly elected on a first past the post basis, to assert its will over a whole people whatever that will may be. It will end in a rigid economic plan, and, I believe, in a siege economy, a curbed and subservient judiciary, and a regulated press. It will impose uniformity on the whole nation in the interest of what it claims to be social justice. It will insist on equality. It will distrust all forms of eccentricity and distinction. It will crush local autonomy. It will dictate the structure, form, and content of education. It may tolerate, but will certainly do its best either to corrupt or destroy, religion. It will depend greatly on caucuses or cadres to exert its will. Some will be directly appointed by patronage as in the increasing number of 'Quangos'. Others will be elected by a tiny minority of dedicated activists and apparatchiks relying on the apathy of the rest as a passport to office. This is already happening in some unions and local authorities. It will worship material values, but not succeed in producing material plenty. When its policies fail, it will rely strongly on class divisiveness or scapegoats to distract attention from its failures.

Among the white races the present apostles of this type of democracy are mainly of the left. In Eastern Europe and in parts of Africa and Asia they have already succeeded in producing 'people's' democracies. In this country they still represent a small minority, though they include Privy Councillors amongst their number. My criticism of them may therefore be resented as the querulous complaints of an ageing Conservative dedicated to the philosophy of a bygone age.

To such critics I will reply that their complacency is misplaced. Centralized democracy is not the prerogative of Socialism or of left-wing extremists. The reappearance of Fascism under the banner of the National Front should sound a warning, and, if history is any guide, such movements will not be sent away simply by abuse or attempts at suppression. The best modern exposition of centralized democracy so far may be 'The British Road to Socialism' issued by the Communist Party of Great Britain. But both Hitler and Mussolini and the various Quislings in Europe were apostles of the same creed. So was Sir Oswald Mosley in Britain. All were spawned from the loins of nineteenth-century Liberalism, and although the progeny was manifestly illegitimate, it was none the less authentic. All these creeds

are the natural offspring of two related humanist philosophies, utilitarianism and legal positivism. The belief of
the first is that the common good is the only criterion of
political action, and that talk of human rights and natural
law or justice to borrow Bentham's luminous phrase is no
more than 'nonsense on stilts'. The exponents of centralized
democracy on the left should pause to reflect that the mirror
image of their political methods and ideals is presented by
the National Front, and their main constitutional dogmas
are supported ever more explicitly as time goes on by Mr
Enoch Powell. Above all, I find it strange that they do not
consider the example of South Africa. Apartheid was illegal
under the entrenched clauses of the old South African
constitution. One nationalist measure after another depriving the coloured community of its rights was struck down
by the Supreme Court. Unhappily, there was one gap. The
Senate was first packed and thereafter the Supreme Court
was by-passed. The doctrine of centralized power had
secured another triumph. If they reflect upon these sinister
examples from the right, left-wingers will, I hope, consider
my presentation of the alternative as something better than
Tory special pleading.

But what is the alternative? I do not present it as a new
thing invented by myself, but it may be that it is novel in
this context. It is the old doctrine inherent from the very
first, that is, from the time of Bracton onwards, in English
Law, that those in a position of political authority may
not rule absolutely, that, being human, even kings may
not place themselves above the law, and may not make
laws which affront the instructed conscience of the com-
monalty. This is the theory of limited government. Hitherto
I have called it the doctrine of freedom under law, and, in
some ways, and in other contexts, it may be the better
name. But it is, I believe, the traditional doctrine of Western
Christendom, indeed also of pre-Christian Western phil-
osophers, running like a golden thread through the thinking
of European writers from Plato onwards. It reached its
peak, I believe, in England in the time of Burke before
Bentham's Utilitarianism, the belief in the greatest happiness
of the greatest number, married the legal positivism of his
friend Austin, whose creed was that the command of the

ruler was all that there was to be said to define the nature of law. From this union sprang all the various political ideologies which have sought to find intellectual justification in the unlimited authority of the state combined with a general benevolent intention described as the common good.

The reason for the growth of centralized democracy is largely historical. For at least three centuries the great question of politics revolved around the relationship between privileged rulers and the unrepresented ruled. During this period Parliament came to be regarded as the guardian of liberty, and the executive as the representative of lawful authority. But the conflict came to an end with the total victory of Parliament at the time of the Act of Settlement. Thenceforward Parliament controlled the executive by way of Cabinet government.

But it did not take long for men to notice that the victorious Parliament was itself unrepresentative based as it was on an uneven franchise, unequal constituencies and a corrupt membership. So began the struggle for a reform of the franchise, attempted during the eighteenth century, interrupted by the French revolutionary wars, achieved to a limited extent by the Reform Bill but pursued thereafter and completed only in my lifetime by the grant of the so-called 'flapper vote' in 1925. If only Parliament could be made to represent the whole adult population, it was argued, abuses would be remedied, injustices expunged, and inequalities abolished. So, at each stage, a proposed extension of the franchise moved hand in hand with the demand for progress.

Since 1925 the demand has been to put into practice the benefits already available in theory. The emphasis has been on welfare and social reform, and, despite recession and world war, much has been achieved, so much indeed that it seemed at first that nothing was amiss. But gradually people have come to realize that all is not well. Our society is not stable. Whole geographical units show signs of wishing to opt out. Organized minorities clamour to be heard, and, what they cannot win by the ballot box, seek to extract by violence or by depriving the population of their rightful needs. In the world of universal franchise, loyalty is at a discount. Self-discipline is a dirty word. Law and order have become objects of ridicule. Every restraint must be removed, and the anarchic total described as liberation, permissiveness, or even humanism. Worst of all, society is divided as never before.

It is only now that men and women are beginning to realize that representative institutions are not necessarily guardians of freedom, but can themselves become engines of tyranny. They can be manipulated by minorities, taken over by extremists, motivated by the self-interest of organized millions. We need to be protected from our representatives no less than from our former masters.

To those who feel the gradual but spreading sense of unease I propound an explanation and offer an alternative. The explanation is that neither legal positivism nor utilitarianism is true. Each fails to satisfy the reason. Neither corresponds with our experience. Above all both affront our sense of justice.

The alternative is the theory of limited government, familiar enough when men could recognize the distinction between government and governed because they were in different hands, but long obscured by anonymous majorities and rising standards of life.

The theory of limited government offers precisely what the dominant theory denies. In place of uniformity it offers diversity. In place of equality it offers justice. In place of the common good, it protects the rights of minorities and the individual. As an alternative to regulation it propounds the rule of law. It does not seek to overthrow governments or institutions, or abolish universal franchise or popular rule. But it prescribes limits beyond which governments and Parliaments must not go, and it suggests means by which they can be compelled to observe those limits. In place of concentrating, it diffuses power. It confers rights of self-government on previously ignored communities. It offers protection against the oppressiveness of unions and corporations.

Above all it corresponds with the general conscience of mankind. While the dominant theory propounds that a bare majority may pass what laws it wills, the doctrine of limited government asserts that individuals and minorities have rights against constituted authority, even when this is elected by universal franchise. Agamemnon was wrong to sacrifice Iphigenia to give a fair wind to the fleet. He would not have done right had he been authorized to do so by popular acclamation, as no doubt he was. Caiaphas spoke falsehood when he asserted that it was expedient that one man should die for the people. He would not have spoken truth even had he a unanimous vote of the Sanhedrin, or the full approval of the majority, as perhaps he did when the crowd yelled for the release of the guilty Barabbas and the crucifixion of the innocent Christ.

We do not put down deformed or defective children as if they were unwanted rabbits. We do not condemn the incapacitated or paralysed old. When lawyers, and judges, and voters, and Members of Parliament communicate with one another and seek to justify their proposals they seldom find it convincing to rely on the general good or the will of the majority. Increasingly they find themselves compelled to use arguments founded on the half-forgotten conceptions of right and wrong, justice and injustice. So the theory of limited government is beginning to re-emerge, and the dominant doctrine of positivism allied to utilitarianism to diminish.

This is the subject which I wish to expound. This is the philosophy of the state I wish to proclaim. This is the doctrine I wish to embody in constructive policies, and a renewed constitutional framework.

II

THE CITY OF DESTRUCTION

For some years now, and especially since February 1974, I have been oppressed by a sinister foreboding. We are living in the City of Destruction, a dying country in a dying civilization, and across the plain there is no wicket gate offering a way of escape. We have to stay here and fight it out. Indeed we must do so for the sake of our children. I do not say the situation is hopeless. Indeed, if I thought so I would not trouble to write. But, if we go on as we are, I can see nothing but disaster ahead, though I am quite unable to predict either when, or exactly how, it will overtake us. There is a deal of ruin in a nation, and a realm can go on decaying for centuries, like Imperial Spain or the Ottoman Empire. What is certain is that one cannot go on for ever borrowing money and spending it on current consumption. However accommodating one's creditors, or however much they may wish to keep one afloat, the day of reckoning will come in the end. One cannot go on indefinitely refusing to face the facts of life. It may be a slow slide to destruction, or it may all end in a big bang. But whimper or bang, slide or sudden explosion, there will come a time, sooner or later, when a nation which has lost its self-respect must face the truth. If it happens sooner, it may extricate itself from its difficulties. If it happens later, it may pass into oblivion, like Imperial Russia, or Austria–Hungary, or re-emerge phoenix like after passing through the fires of revolution or civil war like Kemal Ataturk's Turkey. None of these prospects can be regarded as tolerable to one, like myself, who regards the West as the main hope of the human race, and believes that the fortunes of Britain are critical to the future of the West.

This does not mean that I have abandoned faith in our traditions or institutions. I continue to believe in democracy and wish for more of it rather than less. But the evidence to the contrary is profoundly discouraging. Democracy has a very bad track record. Among forms of human government, it has been the rare exception and, where it has emerged, it has always seemed to carry within it the seeds of its own destruction. It has been short-lived. Even where it has not succumbed to external aggression, it has proved unable to withstand or defend itself against pressures from within, the spendthrifts who disperse its resources, the class warriors who break up its unity, the separatists who try to divide it geographically, the lobbies and pressure groups who try to cajole, corrupt or intimidate its governments, the political parties who undo or undermine each other's activities.

All these factors can be seen at work in Britain since the war, and, in the last few years they have been increasingly successful in making our government ineffective. I say ineffective. Nevertheless, whilst it has become increasingly ineffective, and therefore despised, by a curious paradox, our government has become increasingly oppressive, and therefore hated.

Waiting in the wings are the zealots of world communism, resolutely determined to devour us when the internal contradictions within our society have rendered us incapable of defending ourselves. In the meantime, their influence, and even their dominion, grows wider. By another paradox, whilst it becomes more and more apparent that their ideology is intellectually and morally indefensible, and that even after half a century their policies are incapable of providing their people either with sufficiency of material goods or spiritual happiness, the number of communities they are able to influence is constantly growing in number, and their military preparedness and the proliferation of their weapons increase year by year. They do not need these weapons for defence, for they have never been attacked, and know that no one means to attack them. Nevertheless, they continue to develop these weapons in larger quantities and greater sophistication. Whereas the West attempts to provide aid to the Third World in the shape of economic assistance, the Communist nations provide them with weapons to enable them to carry on hostilities or subversion against their enemies, real or supposed, or against one another, or to hold down their own populations. Beyond the frontiers of the Iron Curtain a vast array of military weapons and formations, nuclear and conventional, is constantly in readiness and as constantly increasing, supported by huge fleets of aircraft, missiles, submarines, and surface craft unexampled in time of peace. All points in a single direction, the melancholy warnings of the Chinese about Soviet intentions, the unanimous testimony of defectors to the West, the failure of repeated efforts to secure disarmament, the continued suppression of dissidents notwithstanding the Helsinki Agreement, the occupation of subject territories. It is all there and the sacred writings of Lenin and Marx and their present-day commentators all confirm the same tale. In the meantime we, unable to make ends meet, are equally unable to achieve the minimum of unity to manage our own affairs.

Nothing less than a complete reassessment of our position would seem necessary to re-establish the credibility of the economic and political values for which we used to believe ourselves to stand. We need to ask ourselves whither we are trying to go. We need to contrast the complete failure of our present-day society to achieve its professed objectives, with the achievements of our past history which it has been fashionable to despise. It is not too late to put our affairs in order. We shall be made the target for external attack only in proportion as our internal differences render us disunited and incapable of, or indifferent to, collective self-defence. In order to render ourselves safe, we have first to recover our self-respect, and to do this we need to achieve some concrete success on however modest a scale. We must identify the causes of our failure and consciously seek to build a political and constitutional framework which will both embody our ideals and enable them to survive in a stable and self-regulating form.

Like my last, this is a book of reflections but, since they relate to contemporary politics, unlike my last they are necessarily controversial, and I am conscious that I shall be accused of bias. If this means that I have either been consciously dishonest or unfair, I plead not guilty. I admit that I hold strong opinions, and that some of my judgements on contemporary events are harsh. But to hold strong opinions is not necessarily to be unfair or even mistaken. I make no secret of my life-long commitment to the Conservative

Party. But, unless Britain is to develop into a single party state, members of parties must not be condemned out of hand. Each is seeking to serve the nation of which he is part, sometimes at a high cost to himself. The reader must make his own judgement of these things. Being largely based on the events of the past four years when a Labour Government was in office, and my own party in opposition, the examples given are, no doubt, to that extent one-sided. But I am myself convinced that a writer from an opposite viewpoint, basing himself on the experience of earlier years, would be driven to the same conclusions, or conclusions at least pointing in the same direction.

My excuse for writing is that I sincerely believe what I am saying, and the opinions expressed are mine and mine alone. I seek to involve no colleagues. I have not consulted them. If what I write is found unacceptable the blame must rest squarely where it belongs, on my own shoulders, and no one else's.

I have not always been of the same gloomy opinion. When I wrote *The Case for Conservatism* in 1947 I was altogether in a different mood. I was writing in the aftermath of the great Labour victory in 1945. It seemed to me then that the existence of the Labour Party was as acceptable in the twentieth as that of the Liberal Party in the nineteenth century. In my eyes the only danger lay in the preponderance of its electoral influence. My aim was to challenge its ideas. But I visualized the continuance of the two-party system with Conservative and Labour alternating between periods of power and opposition, as Liberals and Conservatives had done up to the First World War. I did not look at all for a change in our constitutional arrangements.

By the time the second edition of my book had come out in 1959, my viewpoint had shifted. I was still, as now, a political pluralist. It still does not occur to me to visualize the Conservative or any other party as the only political organization in the state. On the contrary, it seems to me that the kind of society in which I believe can thrive only in the presence of a plurality of parties. But, by 1959, the objectives of 1946 had been very largely achieved. There was no longer any danger that the Conservative Party would disappear or that its principles would be forgotten.

It was indeed once more the leading, if not actually the preponderant, influence in the state.

But, in the meantime, my attitude to the Labour Party had considerably sharpened. It had not, as I had hoped it was going to do under Hugh Gaitskell, adapted itself to a permanent role as one of two great political coalitions, alternating between power and opposition, each content that the other should make its own characteristic and complementary contribution to the common good. On the contrary, and despite Hugh Gaitskell's leadership, it was going more and more irrevocably down the dark alleyways of irreversible and revolutionary change based on its original ideological commitment and class war. The first criticism was proved by its refusal to delete Clause 4 from its constitution.

But the second was more serious in its possible consequences. The whole approach of the Labour movement to politics and the whole thrust of its propaganda were directed to class antagonism, division and class warfare. This was particularly tragic because by this time it had become unnecessary. The social and economic justification for such an attitude had largely disappeared from the actual facts of national life.

Thirdly, and quite apart from the inability of the leadership to control extremism, the organic connection between the Trade Union movement and the Labour Party, justifiable in the early days when financial backing was a necessity if working men were to be maintained in Parliament, seemed to me to be a corrupting and undemocratic factor built into the very structure of the Labour movement, and to present a growing constitutional threat. If political pluralism is to be a reality, it is important that political parties should be independent of control by outside bodies. Of course each must, at least to some extent, reflect the distinctive view and interests of particular sections of the community as the classical Liberal alliance of the nineteenth century largely voiced and reflected the views of nonconformity and manufacturing industry. It is right that political parties, which in Parliament represent the nation in division as well as uniformity, should present and focus the varying attitudes of different economic and social interests as well as different areas and geographical divisions. But I believe that both management and the work force in industry should be free to shop around, as elsewhere in the Western world, in their attempt to secure political objectives, and should not possess a built-in tendency to favour one side permanently at the expense of another. Still less should they possess a political party as a private property owned and manipulated like a feudal fief, or as a holding company owns its subsidiaries by control of the shareholders' meeting.

For these reasons, whilst, in 1959, I was still a strong partisan of the two-party system, I desired to see the Labour Party replaced by a national party free from its ideological commitment to public ownership, liberated from its organic connection with unions and uncontaminated by class warfare. Such a party would be independent, evolutionary, and, up to a point, pragmatic. I do not believe that such a desire was either ignoble or impracticable, still less undemocratic. In 1959 I thought that if we won the election of 1964, as we very nearly did, and might well have done but for the decision to abolish resale price maintenance, that it would have happened. British politics would have then resumed its traditional balance between two principal national coalitions, each with its distinctive part to play in the evolution of this nation and each dominated by the opinions of its moderate wing. The one would have been broadly conservative and pluralist in outlook. The other, equally undogmatic, and not less moderate, would have broadly favoured dirigism and centralization. Though probably on the Conservative side of the dividing line, I would have been somewhere near the point of demarcation. These hopes were dashed as the result of the general election of 1964 and the mistakes made in the previous twelve months. But I was not yet ready to accept the necessity for constitutional change as distinct from a change in the party boundaries.

Since then, it seems to me that the politics of Britain have consistently deteriorated and there can, therefore, be no third edition of *The Case for Conservatism*. The whole framework within which it was written can no longer provide a stable society. It follows that a new dispensation is necessary, and the enquiry as to what this should be forms the main subject matter of this book. In particular, since February 1974, the process seems to me to have accelerated. The old party structure, which for so long guaranteed the evolutionary character of our society, seems to me to have broken down. Although still far removed from the tyrannies on the other side of the Iron Curtain, or the military dictatorships and one-party states so frequent in the Third World, it seems to me that we are moving more and more in the direction of an elective dictatorship, not the less objectionable in principle because it is inefficient in practice, and not the less tyrannical in its nature because the opposed parties, becoming more and more polarized in their attitudes, seek with some prospects of success to seize the new levers of power and use them alternately to reverse the direction taken by their immediate predecessors. All the more unfortunate does this become in the presence of narrow majorities, each representing a minority of the electorate, sometimes a small minority, and when at least one of the parties believes that the prerogatives and rights conferred by electoral victory, however narrow, not merely entitle but compel it to impose on the helpless but un-organized majority irreversible changes for which it never consciously voted and to which most of its members are opposed.

It seems to me that this is a situation the reverse of liberal and even the reverse of democratic, in the sense in which the word has hitherto been understood. Fundamental and irreversible changes ought only to be imposed, if at all, in the light of an unmistakable national consensus. It follows that, if I am right, the overriding need of the moment is to pursue policies and enact legislation to ensure that a like situation to the present is never allowed to recur. It is true that the present nature of the threat can be seen to come from the left. But this need not necessarily be so, and almost certainly it will not always be so. Sir Oswald Mosley's programme of the late thirties proposed to make exactly the same use of the lack of constitutional safeguards as that which I now condemn, and, given a deterioration in our present economic situation, or a racial strife of the type foretold by Mr Enoch Powell, a populist government of the right, taking the place of the present moderate Conservative leadership, might well offer exactly the same threat.

My thesis is that our institutions must be so structurally altered that, so far as regards permanent legislation, the will of the majority will always prevail against that of the party composing the executive for the time being, and that, whoever may form the government of the day will be compelled to follow procedures and policies compatible with the nature of Parliamentary democracy and the rule of freedom under law. I recognize, of course, that many of our present ills are due to errors of economic policy and will not be cured unless these are first reversed. But many, even of these errors, are due at least in part to the form of elective dictatorship imposed by our present constitution and the policies of existing parties. I believe that if we go on as we are going, and as the situation moves from crisis to crisis, our economic maladies will provide the excuse for more and more tyrannical measures, and greater and still greater centralization, until at last a full economic dictatorship with a siege economy may well be the only way of avoiding social and economic collapse. If so, we shall not be the first democracy to fall in this way. It is, in fact, the classical route by which free societies can lose their liberties without defeat in war. It is in fact the road taken first by Italy, and then, successively, by Germany and France in the years between the wars.

Happily the situation is not irremediable. There are still free elections, and one here cannot be long delayed. But this can only be salutary, if, when it comes, the victors, whoever they may be, take the opportunity to do what is necessary to restore a stable economy and to restore the rule of freedom under law.

III

THE ECLIPSE OF BRITAIN

I gave the impression in my last chapter that the evils which need remedy have arisen in an acute form only since October 1964 and, more particularly, since February 1974. But these events must be seen in a historical context. It is this context which gives them their significance, and it is this context which I now wish to examine. It is the context of national decline, some part of which was due to inevitable secular trends, but for some part of which we must all take some share of responsibility.

In 1945, Britain was one of the great powers of the world. We had a million men under arms. We enjoyed the prestige justly due to the only nation which had survived as a belligerent from 1939 without suffering at some time either occupation or military defeat. No one would pretend that in the thirty-three years succeeding VE day we have retained this position, and, whilst making every allowance for the weaknesses of the successive Cabinets which directed our fortunes in this period of national decline, it would be folly to suppose that the fault lay solely with them, or with any group of them. The enquiry in this chapter is not undertaken for the purpose of assessing blame or increasing the area of recrimination. It is rather designed to show that, despite the change in our national status, the decline in our fortunes, and the need to take stock of our institutions, there remain elements in our national tradition which it would be folly to cast away. The purpose of this chapter is to identify some of these and establish their permanent value.

Until recently, the peoples of these islands have been among the most successful political communities in history. For nearly a thousand years we have suffered no successful invasion by a foreign power. Since the Hanoverian succession, we have suffered no serious civil war. We have passed from feudalism to democracy without violent revolution, and without losing the magic of virtually immemorial institutions. These institutions have not only succeeded at home. They have provided the inspiration, and even the models, for other free societies throughout the world.

Nor have our achievements been limited to the domestic field. Without any coherent or conscious desire for universal dominion and with the minimum of force we achieved political sovereignty over a quarter of the earth's surface and inhabitants, and our rule provided a better, fairer and more incorrupt government than had been known before we came, or, I would claim, than the majority have known since we left. Our scientists and inventors largely inaugurated the scientific age. We have pioneered almost every known form of human recreation except polo and chess. We founded the only system of jurisprudence to rival the Roman. Our currency remained virtually unchanged in value for more than a century. 'Made in England'; 'British Made' or 'Home Killed' were guarantees of quality in our shops. No doubt, in matters of what now is called social justice and social conscience, British society was no more farsighted or sensitive than others. But even in this field we were among the pioneers, and there was never any reason to suppose that the institutions which had successfully and peaceably evolved through so many successive changes had exhausted their usefulness or could not have been continued to carry social progress forward through a period of increasing prosperity and material wealth.

In retrospect, it is clear that the First World War and not the Second was the real end of our unrivalled position and the true watershed of our national fortunes. For a long time we hoped, with some reason, for a return to 'normalcy'. In spite of trade recession and unemployment, so late as 1928 or early 1929 these hopes were by no means absurd. Moreover, though the fabric of the Empire had been severely shaken, there was, at that time, no reason to believe that by a steady process of evolution towards self-government and independence, what had been called the *pax britannica* would not continue to preserve the peace of the world, on a basis all the more stable because dependent on general acceptance rather than military force.

Again in retrospect, it is clear that the economic collapse between 1929 and 1931 shattered these hopes. Britain

emerged at the end of the thirties more afraid of unemployment than inflation. The first was a continuing scourge.
From the second we had suffered only to a minor degree.
By contrast, Europe had reason to be more conscious of the
danger of inflation than unemployment. From the misery of
Europe arose the moral disintegration of France, Germany
and Italy. The movement towards the Second World War
had begun. The United States and the Soviet Union could
perhaps have prevented catastrophe. But, each for its own
reasons isolationist, each stood aloof as a mere spectator,
each in its own manner preoccupied with its own problems.

From the Second World War we emerged with our economic and political power shaken, though not yet destroyed.
Yet our reputation, and to some extent our self-esteem, had
never stood at a higher level. Rightly or wrongly, we were
one of the most highly regarded countries in the world, and
this reputation was enhanced rather than diminished by the
sufferings and hardships we had undergone. Better still, of
all the European countries, we were surely the best placed
to achieve a recovery. Our economic rivals were broken,
their fixed capital largely destroyed, their working population,
where it had survived, largely displaced and often in
captivity. Germany was divided into two unequal portions,
each occupied by victors of opposite political tendencies.

What has happened to these hopes? Why have we missed
this opportunity to excel, so obvious, and seemingly so easy
of achievement? Of course, from the start, it was clear that,
relatively speaking, we should be less important than in the
past. Neither the United States nor the Soviet Union, each
emerging from its pre-war isolation, was prepared to tolerate
the continuance of the British Empire. Unhappily, the
means of its disintegration lay ready to hand in the wave of
nationalist feeling and revulsion against European domination which swept the colonial peoples. We had neither the
economic power, nor the political will to resist, and the
result of the headlong rush to autonomy which followed is
that Africa suffers from a brand of dictatorship far more
cruel than the Whitehall bureaucracy, and the Indian sub-
continent, united under Britain but now divided into three
sovereign and independent states, has been shaken by at
least three wars, and has become a pawn in the clash of

wills developing between Russia and China. I do not believe that any of this need have happened had the difficult transition been attempted at a slower pace.

But none of this can excuse our own failure to make the most of our opportunities, our financial imprudence, our loss of self-respect, our failure to effect and consolidate total recovery, our inability to achieve social cohesion or political or economic stability. No secular trend against imperialism can explain our poor performance in comparison with other nations as different as France, Germany, Holland, Belgium, Denmark and Japan. From being the nation best placed to recover, we have progressed the least. We have done badly through our own fault and the sooner we come to realize the fact and to remedy our shortcomings, the better for us and for the rest of the civilized world on whose repeated loans we have come continually to rely in order to shield us from the consequences of our own fecklessness and disunity.

In reaching these harsh conclusions I have no desire whatever to depreciate my own country. On the contrary, my purpose is to arouse a recognition of our faults in order to restore our self-confidence and give us back our self-respect. Yet in the light of what I have just written, it is idle to pretend that the years since 1945 can be regarded without a sense of deep humiliation. Europe and Japan, defeated, ruined and occupied, have picked themselves up, and, with the possible exception of Italy, driven forward to new levels of material prosperity. By contrast, in the last thirty years, we seem to have squandered all our prestige, missed every chance, and fallen behind in almost every field. Norway, Denmark, Belgium, Holland, Luxembourg, France, and above all, Western Germany and Japan, have all had, to a greater or lesser extent, their economic miracles. Starting far behind, they have all outstripped us, and they have done so not merely in abstract economic statistics but in the very fields in which we were most apt to pride ourselves, the level of wages, the width and extent of social benefits, the capacity to assist less fortunate countries, the stability of their currencies, and last, but not least, the ability and determination to defend themselves. This they have achieved despite economic policies widely different from one another.

Germany, with its highly devolved federal system, has been very largely inspired by the ideals of free enterprise, and, until recently, even of *laissez-faire*. France, with its tradition of centralized control has been relatively dirigiste. In Denmark, Norway and the Netherlands differing forms of political and social outlooks prevail. But they all have done better than Britain.

The one encouraging feature is that because our humiliation has occurred through our own fault, it is equally within our power to put things right. If the rest of Europe and Japan could pick themselves up and dust their trousers after the collapse of 1945 then so can we who are so infinitely better placed to do so now than they were then. But, if we are to do so, we need to make a conscious effort. We must identify and remedy the causes of our national failure. We need an absolutely unfaltering determination to allow neither sentimentality nor an obsession with purely ideological considerations to stand in the way of national recovery. Our formula must be that everything necessary to secure that object, however disagreeable, must be done, and that everything, however attractive or inherently desirable, which does not serve it must be deferred.

IV

WHAT MAKES A NATION?

In 1946, I felt a need to restate the case for patriotism. I did not feel it necessary to ask 'What makes a nation?'. Yet, without a feeling of national identity there is nothing to feel patriotic about. I was myself, and remain, a British nationalist. But this ideal is no longer treated as self-evidently desirable. There are those who wish to bail out, with varying degrees of popular support. There are others to whom class loyalties, or ideological affinities, are claimed as more important than love of country, or loyalty to fellow countrymen. I question these ideals, and wish to rekindle the old spirit of national consciousness, unity and self-confidence. Whether I be right or wrong about this, it is quite clear that Britain will never recover if Britain cannot command the self-sacrifice and loyalty of her citizens. If we cannot achieve this, we had far better divide into a series of separate communities or merge into some larger entity, which can command the right kind of enthusiasm. Without vision of this kind, the people will surely perish.

A nation is always a compound of different elements. None is decisive. Cyprus and Palestine are not nations, although occupying single and relatively small definable areas. Nor is Ireland, for since 1921 Ireland has been divided between two separate communities and two states. The existence of a common language is far from decisive. The Arabic-speaking world has never been able to unite. Nor would anyone claim that Australia and New Zealand, though speaking English, form a single nation either with one another or with us. A class structure is not incompatible with nationhood. Nor are great differences in wealth. In 1914 British society was markedly divided into social classes, far more so than we are now. At the same time we were a nation and far more united than today. Identity of religion or language is obviously a help, but Switzerland has remained united for centuries despite wide differences in both.

Nationhood is thus clearly to some extent a matter of degree. It seems incapable of purely artificial propagation. Yet patriotism can be engendered where the climate and soil are propitious. This is a paradox. But it can be said with confidence that without a sense of nationhood a people cannot prosper, and that a people which does possess this sense can hardly fail to do so. I believe we had this sense of solidarity in 1914 and 1939. It has to be proved that we have it still.

Yet surely it is obvious that, if there was a case for national unity in 1914 or 1939, it is infinitely stronger in 1977. In 1914, Britain was highly stratified. I am old enough to remember the society of those days, the infinitely small money wages paid, the pitifully inadequate medical care, the terrible power of dismissal or eviction, the fear of an impoverished old age, the condition of housing, the enormous difference created by the possession of rank and income-yielding property, the class consciousness at every level. All this has disappeared. It is no good trying to persuade a man of my age that the country is still riddled with class distinction. He knows better. He can remember. It is no good academic socialist economists claiming to cite statistics purporting to show that differences in wealth are as great as ever. In every real sense class distinctions as we knew them then have almost gone. The statistics take no account of the vast provision of public services, the educational opportunities, the security provided by national insurance and the health service, the catastrophic decline in the living standards of the middle and professional class, the huge rise in the living standards of the wage earners, the underlying safety net of supplementary benefit. Statistics also take no account of the increasing homogeneity of culture brought about by the press, the radio, and the television, and even by popular advertisements. This is not to deny the existence of vulnerable groups, the one-parent families, the physically and mentally handicapped, the under-housed and, in conditions of less than full employment, those who are actually out of work or threatened with unemployment. But these are small matters compared with what I remember in my youth.

Yet it is precisely in the face of this dramatic shift towards classlessness that the class warriors are more vocal than ever before and appear to attract more numerous adherents to their divisive creed. There is less class distinction than ever before, less advantage in the possession of wealth, and smaller differences in real income. Yet it is precisely in these circumstances that the ideologists of the left are most shrill in their denunciation of what they are pleased to call social injustice. It is not enough, apparently, that public services should be adequate and poverty eliminated. Uniformity is to be imposed by law, either as an immediate reform, or as an ultimate ideal. Parents are to be forbidden to pay for the education of their children and within the system of provided education, only one kind of school is to be permissible in the whole country, despite the wishes of parents, the votes of local electors, the threat of falling standards, the manifest differences in the aspirations and talents of the children, and despite the growing evidence of bullying and lawlessness in the vast units which the prescribed formula demands. Patients are to be forbidden to pay for their own medical treatment. Private wards in hospitals are to be closed. Doctors are threatened with confinement to the health service. All this is to be done from the centre in the name of social justice. But what if freedom of choice is essential to social justice? What if equality is the antithesis of justice? And what if uniformity imposed from the centre is the most fertile cause of social disruption? What if diversity in unity is the best recipe for unity among a diverse and free-thinking people composed of educated men and women? What if the ideal of classlessness, if it is to mean a compulsory set of values universally imposed, is incompatible either with freedom or the rule of law?

It is impossible to read the literature of the extreme left, or indeed of the more articulate of trade union officials, without realizing that they are wholly blind to the importance of certain elements in the community, particularly the providers of services. The designer, the salesman, the doctor, the small shopkeeper, the self-employed, even the farmer, are consistently undervalued, the things which give them hope, the springs of their action and vitality are systematically eliminated and destroyed, and when by their apathy or deliberate attempts to evade a law which they see as unjust they are seen to revolt, they are denounced as unpatriotic enemies of society. It is strange that the very elements which demand the outlawry of discrimination on the grounds of race or sex are absolutely blind to the disruptive effects of the class war of which they are the principal advocates and practitioners. Yet, so far as I know, no society has ever been disrupted by sex discrimination however deplorable it may be, and however much one may condemn injustice towards immigrant minorities, disruption from this source must be of limited character at the worst. What destroys a nation most completely is disruption which has at its root hatred engendered between the main groups of its permanent inhabitants, and what pulls it together is a deliberately contrived policy of unity designed to emphasize points of identity of interest, and the maximum freedom to practise diversity.

The argument of this chapter is that if we are to get out of our national difficulties, we must restore our national spirit and to do this we need to make class consciousness and class antagonism socially unacceptable. We need to restore respect for the social utility of classes at present left out in the cold. We need to welcome all these back into the bosom of the national community and to give them hope and the sense of being wanted. We need consciously to bring them back into the social contract, a word I use in its original sense, for I mean the unspoken rule of social harmony which alone can make a free political society possible. We need to restore the concept of limited government which makes it possible for coherent minorities to exist within a single society undivided in spite of diversity. We need to accept and encourage social as well as political pluralism. We need to adapt our thinking over policies, and our political institutions in such a way as to make a single nation possible within the wide and embracing shelter of tolerance under a liberal law. But this means an end to imposed uniformity whether by political, fiscal or social pressure. The whole history of the Weimar Republic in Germany and the Third Republic in France proclaims the dreadful danger caused to a modern democracy by an alienated middle class. No doubt the forgotten and under-represented groups which I have described would be prepared now as in the past to undergo great hardships and suffer real privations if they could be offered a little hope for the future, or if they could be persuaded of the present necessity for the discrimination against them. But when they look abroad and see the countries which have pursued lines of policy entirely the opposite of those followed by their own government to be enjoying more growth, better housing, better benefits, more stable currency and higher wages than their own, and even having to lend our own country money in order to stave off recurrent economic collapse, it is obvious either that sooner or later they will revolt altogether and transfer their allegiance by emigration to some other nation, or their loyalty to some political regime in their own country which breaks away in a startling fashion from the political orthodoxy of the past half century.

V

WHAT IS DEMOCRACY?

We sometimes talk as if democracy were a single, easily recognized type of political community. A moment's reflection will show that this is not so. Even amongst those societies which liberally minded people would recognize as democratic there is an enormous range of alternative types, and each possible variation might be a critical factor in determining success or failure. Though no liberal thinker would recognize them as such, outside the group of true democracies an even wider range of nations claim to be democratic. We have no right to speak of democracy unless we define what we mean by it, and, even when we have done so we have no right to assume that everything democratic is good, or likely to succeed in practice. Our cult of democracy must not lead us to ignore questions common to all types of political organization. We must consider whether there are not inherent limitations, moral and practical, on the nature of government itself, whether there are not rights of individuals and minorities, which cannot be ignored even in a democracy. Besides these questions, it is necessary to consider the practical utility of different sorts of democratic institutions, and even questions like optimum size and federation. If we ignore questions like these, we shall allow the name of democracy to continue to be used as a cloak for every kind of abomination and folly, blatant tyranny, incompetent bureaucracy, industrial blackmail, social oppression.

In this discussion I shall use the expression 'Democracy' to mean a statement about political sovereignty and nothing else. I believe this to be its only proper use. Sovereignty can reside in an individual, a selected number of citizens or the whole adult population. Only the last named can be properly called a democracy, and even there the question may be one of degree since powers of sovereignty can be shared, or exercised in practice by organized groups of varying size.

Even so, however understood, the word 'democracy' tells us nothing about the wisdom of policies pursued, or their justice. It reveals nothing of the structure or size of governments, or the nature of institutions, and the relation between them. It does not prescribe the kind of society it protects, the code of morals it enforces, the methods of production distribution or exchange it adopts. Thus even if we do not misuse the word to the extent current on the other side of the Iron Curtain, we can learn little about the prospects for success, the mutual adjustments of social groupings or the distribution of influence or power from the mere fact that a society is a democracy. We know only that over a period the policies pursued, the institutions, the economic structure, and the whole business of laws and law making will be maintained or altered according to the wishes of the whole adult population. All the other matters, so vital to success or failure, justice or injustice, will vary almost indefinitely from case to case. Should the executive, legislature or judiciary be separate, as in the United States or should the executive and the legislature be fused, as in Britain? Should the state be unitary or federal and in what cases? How wide should be the powers of government? What should be the method of voting? To what extent, if at all, should religion, and, if so what religion, be recognized, tolerated or established? Should there be one or two chambers in the legislature? What right of secession or independence should be accorded to subordinate parts? Should military service be compulsory or voluntary? To what extent should there be freedom of speech and association? All governments, democratic and otherwise, must find answers to these questions, more satisfactory or less, and it is a pure illusion to suppose that answers will be forthcoming by the mere repetition of the word 'democracy' as if it were an incantation against the evil eye, or that if a democracy finds answers which are either wrong in principle or unsuitable to its particular condition it will avoid the kind of penalty which would be suffered by a monarch or some other political organization which had made the same mistakes. Democracy is a statement about the centre of gravity where sovereignty resides and to which the ultimate appeal should be made. It is nothing else.

On the whole, democracies have not a good record of success. They have been the exception rather than the rule. Their life has tended to be short, their decline rapid, their policies vacillating, and their economic record not particularly impressive. They have proved among the least enduring of institutions. Yet who would trade ancient Sparta or Corinth or the Persian Empire and all its satrapies for Periclean Athens for all its short life, its sad decline into chauvinism and its disastrous end? Or who would have exchanged Carthage for Rome as mistress of the Mediterranean? Like Winston Churchill, one is tempted to deride democracy until one contemplates the alternatives.

There is a case for saying that democracies have done little more than capture control of an existing political apparatus which they have then contrived to use in the manner of their former masters but for different purposes and with different results. In Britain, democracy took over the medieval structure of parliament and monarchy. Successive French republics did not abandon the centralized control of the kings, as reorganized under Napoleon. Moscow which claims in some sense to be a democracy continues to operate the machine of Peter the Great, even when it has not reverted to that of Ivan the Terrible. More than they know or than we admit, the military dictatorships which have taken over Africa are operating the system of colonial rule learned from the British, with prohibited immigrants, political detention, and bureaucratic control. Political traditions are more easily taken over than created, and the type of sovereignty operated within a territory does not necessarily alter with the identity of the sovereign.

So far as I am concerned, the type of government I favour does not depend on the identity of the sovereign, though I believe that it is more easily attained and perpetuated under a democratic sovereignty than any other. The ideals I aim at could in principle be the mark of any government. I believe in freedom under law, freedom limited by a sense of moral responsibility under a law defined by reference to moral principles as well as utilitarian convenience. No doubt this is best achieved by means of a representative government elected by universal franchise. But the converse is not equally true. Survival will be ensured only if democracy observes the same kind of limitations and restraints which a wise authoritarian government would have to pursue if it truly governed in the interests of the people. If it does not respect these limits it will disintegrate, and, if it abandons them, it will become every bit as odious and foolish as an authoritarian regime pursuing the same lines of policy. The popular vote is a legitimate exercise of sovereignty, but does not mitigate folly or excuse incompetence, still less justify tyranny or injustice on the part of the sovereign. It is simply a statement about the centre of gravity where sovereignty and ultimate responsibility reside, and does not constitute a licence to exercise arbitrary power.

This means that if we wish to justify what we do at any moment of time we cannot simply invoke the sacred name of democracy. We have to go back to older and more traditional criteria of excellence than are popular today. I wish to consider a few of these because I think them undervalued. I give them labels, conscious always that labels may be misleading. But I point in particular to the need to recognize limitations to the rights of government. I label this the theory of limited government. I point to the need to recognize the rights both of individuals and minorities so far as each are prepared to recognize their corresponding responsibility to others. I label this the need for a plural society. I point to the need, proven as it seems to me, for societies to evolve by a process of continuous adaptation, rather than to aim at conformity to a rigid series of ideological conceptions. I label this the theory of continuous evolution, and I contrast it with the various forms of ideology, fascist, communist, or merely eccentric, littered about the world today. Politics, it seems to me, must take into account the fallibility of human nature, the impermanence and incompleteness of all political philosophies, and the inability of man to see far into the future. Politics, however, is neither simply the art of the possible, nor the rule of the majority. It is an art as well as a science. It can afford to ignore neither the practicalities nor the enduring values of human life.

VI

THE NATIONAL PARTIES

Political parties are no part of our constitution, but no part of our constitution can ignore their existence. Governments, parliaments, and local authorities could hardly work without them. Something therefore must be said about them in any account of our constitutional arrangements.

The Labour Party is and always has been a coalition between two groups with inconsistent aims, those whose objective is to remove the blemishes they see, or think they see, in the present structure of society, and those whose aim is altogether to destroy the existing structure and substitute something different. Both groups would regard themselves as socialists and democrats, though they do not always so regard one another, and both groups would describe their aim as socialism, though in fact their two purposes are wholly inconsistent with one another. Both groups have always existed, although, until the advent of Mr Wilson as leader, the right-wing has usually been predominant. Their existence, their incompatibility, and the predominance until recently of the right-wing are well described by the Communist Party of Great Britain in 'The British Road to Socialism' when it speaks of 'right-wing Labour Governments who see their job as making capitalism work' and the two wings as 'the left and broadly socialist trend, and the right-wing trend, accepting capitalism, which has been dominant throughout its (the Labour Party's) existence'. There has always been tension between the two trends but, since Mr Wilson's leadership, this has become more obvious and increasingly bitter.

Although the right-wing has been predominant, the sacred scriptures of the Labour Party, and in particular its formal constitution and its propaganda, have largely favoured the left. So long as it adheres to the rigid formula of Clause 4 of the constitution of the party and states among its objectives the common ownership of all the means of production, distribution and exchange it can never be described, as the Communists do, as 'accepting capitalism', and so long as it continues in organic relationship with the trade unions, it can never rest wholeheartedly democratic. Worse still, its constant forays into class warfare, its misrepresentation of the class structure, its discriminatory legislation and penal tax proposals drive it constantly along the path of centralized democracy, and the economic consequences of these tendencies are not exactly conducive to prosperity, growth, or industrial efficiency.

Towards the Liberal Party my attitude is wholly different. My difficulty about the Liberals is that I believe they have failed to understand the radical difference which the political conditions of the twentieth century impose on persons of liberal outlook. Churchill was amongst the first to diagnose the true position after the First World War. Throughout the nineteenth century the struggle of radicalism in politics was to achieve equality through extension of the franchise, and an abolition of the complicated differences in status of our highly traditional society. There was no drive against the possession of wealth as such. On the contrary, the debate was between freedom and established authority and privilege, and the political divide reflected the attitudes of individuals and organized interests towards this central question. This made the Liberal Party of those days the champion of enhanced freedom and placed them firmly on the political left. So Liberals naturally represented organized nonconformity in religion against the Church by law established, and the new industrial society against the landed interest.

But the challenge of the twentieth century is altogether different. In our days the challengers of the established order are the collectivists. Their challenge is socialism, and this consists of two quite separable parts. One demands publicly organized social services. With this, though there is plenty of room for disagreement in detail, and though I strongly support the right of individuals and minorities to contract out, I am in broad agreement. But the other part stands for an all-pervasive state, owning in particular all the means of production, distribution, and exchange. To this view Conservatives, and myself in particular, are in complete opposition. We do not favour a totally privately owned economy, since such a monster has never existed, and never will or can exist. We favour a mixed economy evolving naturally but with a marked bias against state intervention. In the perennial battle between liberty and authority, which, after all, has always been the main theme of politics in a Western society, the libertarian is on the defensive in the twentieth, as he was on the attack, and held the initiative, in the nineteenth century. This is why conservatives (for this purpose with a small 'c'), who were the natural enemies of the liberals in the nineteenth century, are, or rather should be, their natural allies in the twentieth. The actual organization of parties is partly the consequence of our voting system. It may be that we need two, three, or four separately organized national parties in this country, one or more of which may choose to label themselves conservative or liberal. But there is not room for more than one challenge on the left, and ever since the end of World War I, which is the real boundary line between nineteenth- and twentieth-century politics, the challenge on the left has been from socialism. This the Liberal Party has never properly understood and, instead of realizing that they are now a party on the right, they have striven unsuccessfully to regain the position on the left which has been taken from them by the Labour Party. This is the reason why they have never thriven except during periods in which the Conservative Party has been in office and therefore increasingly unpopular, and why, whenever the Labour Party has been in office they have always suffered disaster. They have never realized that they can never again form a party of the left, and, as a result, have always attempted the impossible.

Their greatest mistake between the wars was when they left the National Government on the issue of tariffs, an issue which, in the politics of the time, was long since dead. If they had stayed inside the administration, not only would they have influenced policy, perhaps decisively, but the Conservatives would have been compelled to support them in most of their constituencies, and they would have bred up a race of liberal statesmen with experience of office, and so gained stature and real credibility. In the last ten years, the period of accelerated national decline with which I am principally concerned, the Liberals have again made the mistake of thinking that they could oust the Labour Party as the party of the left. This was the underlying reason for their failure to take advantage of the Heath offer of a coalition in February 1974. If they had accepted, they would now have a number of safe seats, and three or four ex-Cabinet Ministers, and a few more with minor government experience. As it is, the threat of annihilation has driven them into a temporary alliance with Labour, when they stand to reap all the unpopularity of Labour Government if it fails, and, if it succeeds enjoy none of the rewards of its renewed acceptability.

I now turn to my own, the Conservative Party. I am often asked what would have happened had I succeeded in the leadership selection in 1963. This is not a question which it is possible to answer, since it did not happen, and as no one can be a judge in his own cause I am the last person to attempt to do so. All that is known is what actually has happened since 1963. We have lost four elections out of five. We lost the first in 1964, and we would not, I believe, have lost it, had we not committed the mistake of pursuing the abolition of resale price maintenance, when we could only summon a majority of one for it in the Commons. We only needed about another 250,000 votes in the whole country to win in 1964, at least by a narrow margin, and if we had won that election, the whole sequence of events between 1964 and 1970 would have been avoided. It might very well be that the Labour Party would have split up under the impact of a fourth defeat. None of the nationalization measures adopted since 1964 would have taken place, and Britain might well have entered Europe as a stable mixed economy. Dogmatic socialism would have been left behind, and a new line of demarcation between the parties would have been drawn. On the left of the line might have stood a new social democratic party on the German model, on the right a moderate party of so-called Christian Democrats. We might even have avoided the separatism of Scottish and Welsh nationalism, and most of the successive devaluations of the pound. Whatever the results of elections after 1964 they would have been fought about rival programmes far more pragmatical and less ideological than those evolved respectively at the Selsdon meeting and the successive party conferences of the Labour Party. In my experience, now going back over fifty years, programmes designed in opposition are seldom practical, and, unless left flexible, are almost always abandoned after the assumption of office in circumstances of maximum humiliation.

Whatever the value of these speculations, it seems to me that, despite a considerable lead in popular opinion, the Conservative Party is still far weaker than when Mr Macmillan left office. It has fewer front benchers with actual experience of government and some of its distinguished younger figures are excluded from participation by their convictions on policy. Unless the rift is closed this could prove a serious handicap on a return to office.

More serious than personal disagreements is the widespread popular belief that Conservatives cannot deal with the unions. This has almost become part of political mythology, and though it is wholly false, the fact that it is widely held makes it almost as dangerous as if it were true. The legend has grown despite one very obvious fact. This is that, during the thirteen years between 1951 and 1964 when the Conservatives were continuously in power, relations between government and unions were seldom better, despite the unions' relationship with the Labour Party, and despite the fact that, on the whole, wage increases, although excessive, were nothing like so large as in the disastrous twelve months after 1974.

The reason why the legend has grown has been largely for reasons the true bearing of which is misunderstood. To begin with, coal mining is one of the very few activities which cannot be done by anyone else. There is no means by which public opinion can have a strong effect on the miners who largely live in a self-contained world of their own, and, under nationalization, a battle with a united miners' union can only be fought effectively by a House of Commons with a firm government majority, a public opinion which is prepared to bear the hardship and expense of prolonged industrial conflict, and an economy which can continue to function without the mines. In 1974 Mr Heath's Government were advised that the slender majority in the House would not prove solid without a new contact with the electorate. We should, I believe, have won the 1974 election but for three unfortunate events which had nothing to do with the case, and with which I have dealt elsewhere. Had we done so there is little doubt that we could have made a settlement acceptable to the miners probably at least marginally more favourable to the economy than that achieved under Sir Harold Wilson's leadership which was based on total surrender. If this had been achieved many of the consequences of the Wilson settlement on the general level of wages would probably have been avoided. The idea that the miners' demands had anything to do with the Industrial Relations Act 1971, or any of its provisions, does not really bear examination. No doubt the heat engendered had a distinct psychological effect. But this had little to do with the miners at all or with our defeat at the election. The Act was popular when it was passed, and public opinion had all along rejected union opposition. The three-day week provided an immense and valuable opportunity to illustrate how great an increase in productivity can be achieved when management and the work force are on the same side. I was myself highly critical of the policy which led to the Industrial Relations Act 1971 at the time when it was devised in opposition. Parts of it were good, but the whole project was far too ambitious for a single Act of Parliament, and it sought to combine at least two separate objectives, which had better been secured separately, namely the rationalization of industrial relations in the light of the changed and improved status of the unions and the introduction of a law conferring on unions the same position in a codified law as that occupied in a quite different field by limited companies. In fact the latter objective has been largely retained by the present government, but by the use of technical terminology designed to conceal its purpose. The recognition of the new status and responsibility of unions has not been achieved. Instead, the legislation of 1974 and 1975 taken together, so far from simply repealing the Conservative Act, is in some ways completely reactionary, and is already producing the symptoms of mob rule and industrial chaos.

The fact is, however, that, political propaganda being what it is, the Conservative Party needs to take particular care to do nothing to corroborate the legend, and ought wherever possible to take special steps to destroy it. The financial situation is likely to be so serious that any government will almost certainly have to take a series of harsh and unpalatable decisions. Public expenditure now disposes of much more than half our national product. In these conditions, prices, particularly of food, are bound to rise, and any government on taking office is certain to face a good deal of public hostility arising out of trends which are really inevitable. In the background ugly forces, of which avowed Communists are only one, and perhaps the least dangerous example, are eager to take advantage of the situation to destroy our mixed economy altogether and with it the ideals and values of a free society.

My own advice to the party leaders of either side is not likely to be taken, but it is this. Though coalition may be undesirable, and, in the absence of a parliamentary situation requiring it is certainly impossible, each of the major parties needs to broaden its political and social base. The Labour Party cannot govern on the basis of the organized male factory vote alone. The Conservative Party cannot govern on the basis of the self-employed, the professional classes, middle management, and agriculture alone. Each party should seek to understand, and to bring to its own side some at least of the classes and interests most likely normally to vote for the other. Butskellism has become a dirty word among professional politicians, and in so far as it implies an attempt to avoid facing choices or to compromise or delay between two or more incompatible decisions I accept this judgement. But dogmatism and doctrinaire ideology are not necessarily either attractive or realistic political qualities. If democracy, which demands a change of government from time to time, is condemned for ever to oscillate between two factions with opposing philosophies rigidly applied, I cannot see much prospect for its future. There may be courses which are acceptable to each set of principles, or dictated by the nature of the case rather than by ideologies. Pragmatism and moderation are themselves political principles and in an uncertain and changing situation not to be despised as indications of weakness or indecision. Even the dictates of ideology have to be placed in a strict order of chronological priority or subordinated for a time altogether to practical needs. I suspect that Mr Callaghan understands this better than Mr Wilson. I trust that my own colleagues may understand it equally well.

Were I in charge of any of the three political parties, for the reasons I have already given, I would not aim at a coalition. I would play to win. But when I had won and had a firm majority at my back in the House of Commons I would strive to invite into my government anyone of sufficient distinction or experience to hold high office who was willing to serve in it in either House of Parliament, and I would plan my policies accordingly. I would not unnecessarily bait my defeated opponents or antagonize their supporters. Were I a leader of the Liberals I would not reject overtures from the leaders of other parties more successful than my own, but, contrary to what appears to be the ruling tradition in that party, I would demand office, both for myself and my colleagues as a condition of my support, even though that support was that of a minority party whose presence in the government was not strictly necessary to give it a majority. Both the leadership and the back-bench membership of all parties should seek contact with the others if only to try and understand their legitimate feelings and aspirations and to see how far these aspirations might be met without compromise of essential principles and policies. Political angularity is not necessarily the same thing as political integrity. When I was at the Bar, I always found it to my client's advantage to be personally on good terms with my opponent, and although I had my share of rows with individuals, I always regarded these when they occurred as a misfortune and not an advantage either to myself or my client. I believe this is the wisdom of the professional advocate, inherited over generations, and I believe that here at least politicians would be wise to take a leaf out of the advocate's book. Politics can be a dirty business, but there is no reason why it should be so, and I do not myself think that hard hitting in controversy is in any way compromised by showing the chivalry and generosity which one would hope to receive oneself. If we are to escape from the City of Destruction, the political victors, whoever they turn out to be, will have to show great sagacity and leadership and continue to command the central conscience of the nation in their journey across the plain.

VII

THE FAILURE OF PARTY POLITICS

In the eclipse of Britain, one, at least, of the salient factors has been our failure to manage our economic affairs. It is the purpose of this chapter to show that this failure is due, at least in part, to the breakdown of the party system on whose implied conventions the due working of our constitution depended.

Of course I write from a Conservative point of view. But the conclusion does not differ greatly from that reached by many who argue from Socialist premises. Only the other day, as I write this, I recall that Mr Benn said expressly that, in his view at least, there was no more possibility of compromise. The country, he said, must choose between what he described as the capitalist system and the brand of thorough-going socialism which he favoured. I disagree with this view because I do not believe that there exists, except in the minds of some theorists, a system which can be referred to as the capitalist system with any degree of precision and still less is there any defined meaning to the expression 'Socialism'. The real choice which I believe has to be made in the not too distant future is between some kind of authoritarian state, more probably, though not necessarily, one of the left, based on ideology, and the national tradition of alternating governments, evolving policies, pragmatic choices, and unspoken conventions. In my own terminology the choice is between elected dictatorship and limited government.

I agree with Mr Benn that the party system has, temporarily at least, broken down, and my purpose is to analyse the cause of its failure and to identify, if possible, the means whereby it can be put back on its feet.

The traditional system depended largely on conventions. While parties might fight theoretical battles over their principles, none pressed them to the length of imposing an ideology of its own in a rigid or unalterable form on the entire nation. None pressed a narrow electoral advantage too far. Though many changes were made in the course of the evolutionary process which in fact proved irreversible and even revolutionary in their consequences (the Reform Act of 1832 was an example), such changes were in fact adopted when it had been clearly shown, both that they were demanded by an overwhelming weight of public opinion outside Parliament, and that the decisive steps taken at any stage were deliberate, practicable and reasonable.

It seems to me that, since the war, except during the period of Conservative Government between 1951 and 1964, these assumptions have ceased to be made. I agree with Mr Benn, though with an opposite assessment of its desirability, that a principal cause of this is the composition and structure of the party to which he belongs.

To do it justice, the Labour Party has never been, and has never pretended to be, the same sort of institution as the old Liberal and the present Conservative Parties. I had hoped at one time that it might become such a party in course of time and with the experience of power. In fact, this has not happened. On the contrary the Labour Party has remained another sort of entity altogether, committed to an ideology, structurally assimilated to the Trade Union movement, and committed to the class struggle. The result has been to polarize opinion and to render impossible any consistent growth in national consciousness. The Liberals are right in describing the recent alternation of dominant parties as a see-saw, and condemning it as undesirable. The problem as I see it is to identify this polarization as a major cause of our troubles and to find a way out which is compatible with the prescriptions for national spirit and democracy which I have sought to define.

I wish to disclaim at once the view that political parties forfeit their claim to be national by seeking to reflect particular interests. The purpose of politics in a free society is to focus public attention on possible alternative courses of action in a given situation. It is, therefore, not only not disreputable but positively commendable for parties to reflect in differing degrees the general outlook of particular

47

social groupings. Thus in the nineteenth century it was commendable in the Liberal Party to reflect the attitude of the free Churches and the manufacturing interest, and the Conservatives to look to the country, the aristocracy and the Church as regular bases for support. Parties lose touch with reality when they become purely ideological groupings. By the end of the century it became clear that, though each had competed for the support and appealed to the needs of the urban wage earners, there was room for a party based more specifically on their interests and needs. Unfortunately, however, the actual constitutional structure of the Labour Party as it has evolved drives it into attitudes which render it almost impossible either in office or in opposition to pursue genuine national objectives. To begin with, Clause 4 of its constitution, which Hugh Gaitskell sought to eliminate, compels it to an open-ended commitment to expropriate private ownership in all (yes, all) the enterprises engaged in manufacture, distribution and exchange. Over the whole of my adult life this has been a permanent source of uncertainty inhibiting productive investment in industry and an obvious encouragement to short-term speculation. Other social democratic parties on the continent have long since disregarded such a commitment, where it existed, and have, in consequence, enjoyed long periods of influence and office. Only in Britain has the social democratic party stuck to this tribal totem, not simply as a matter of ritual veneration, but of practical politics. The effect is to drive the movement more and more into the camp of the class warriors. All those who own shares or businesses tend to be their natural enemies and become in due course permanent targets for their attacks. It also leads to an immense element of hypocrisy, since most Labour leaders have expensive tastes and considerable personal fortunes.

So far as I know, the British Labour Party is nearly the only social democratic party in Europe apart from Scandinavia which maintains an organic connection between the party as organized in Conference and the constituencies and the Trade Union movement. This is a very different thing from their being a party broadly representative of organized labour. The Labour Party is owned by the unions going to make up the TUC in exactly the same sense as a subsidiary company is owned by a holding company. Their sovereign body is the conference. The votes in the conference do not depend on one man, one vote, but are cast in proportion to the number of members belonging to the affiliated organizations. The TUC affiliated unions control four-fifths of the votes, and, where they agree, can therefore control the conference. Where they do not agree, the individual card votes can be bartered in exchange for particular promises and undertakings. When it comes to finance, four-fifths of the funds are raised from similar sources, and, since they come indirectly from relatively small contributions exacted from members unless they expressly contract out of their obligation to pay into the political funds, this puts a great deal of power into the hands of the apparent chiefs of the organization. Historically, no doubt, this system made it possible for wage earners to promote candidates truly representative of their cause for a Parliament whose members were largely unpaid. In a mature party seeking to be one of the main parties in a Parliamentary democracy neither feature is healthy. It puts far too much power in the hands of trade union officials who are in turn elected by a small fraction of their potential electorate, and it causes trade unions to regard the Labour Party as a sort of feudal fief and to promote its short-term interests when the true interest both of the trade unions and of the class they represent is to maintain a degree of independence. I am not, of course, arguing that there is anything wrong in either a company or a union voting money in support of political purposes or of a political party. What I do believe, and what Lord Poole and I studiously insisted on maintaining whilst we were responsible for Conservative affairs, is that the money, when subscribed, should have no direct strings attached. In the last resort a party must be ruled by its members and have a real independence of its subscribers. But this is exactly what is not true of the Labour Party. The sovereign body is controlled, and the political organization is financed by the same people. Even a high proportion of their MPs are similarly sponsored or subsidized. I do not believe that in the long run this is compatible with good democratic practice.

49

Incidentally, I do not believe that the unions themselves are organized in such a way as to promote stability or industrial efficiency. But that is another aspect of the matter. What I am at present concerned to discuss is the extent to which these theoretical weaknesses have contributed to the eclipse of Britain.

In my lifetime there have been four complete periods of Labour Government, in 1923–4, in 1929–31, in 1945–51, in 1964–70. At the time of writing, the fifth, which began in February 1974, is still incomplete. In each case, the history of these administrations seems to have followed a similar pattern. This is true of all five periods, though of course I am aware that the two pre-war Labour Governments did not command a majority of the House of Commons, and the second was overtaken by a world recession for which it could not be regarded as wholly or perhaps even largely responsible. Nonetheless the similarity of pattern remains striking. The party assumes power from a Conservative administration which has lost popularity. It comes into office shackled by a policy dictated partly by the conference, partly by pledges given and attitudes acquired in opposition, and partly by the terms of the election manifesto. These all involve relatively enormous outlays of public money mainly directed at current consumption. There follows a period of honeymoon in which part at least of the programme is put into effect, a larger part if the majority is adequate, a smaller part if it is marginal, or if the government has to depend on Liberal support. Since more radical measures need time to draft and prepare, the part of the programme involving increased public expenditure carried into effect during the honeymoon period is relatively large. After a short period of time (in 1964 it was about six weeks, and in 1974 it was less) this increase in current expenditure or commitment to current expenditure leads either to financial stringency or to a marked degree of inflation. The price level and the stability of the currency is threatened, and resort is therefore had to borrowing at home and abroad and higher taxes. In so far as the borrowing is from abroad, there is a progressive loss of independence to foreign creditors. In so far as the borrowing is from internal sources, this and the higher taxes reduce the funds from which productive investment can be made, and thereby the competitive effectiveness of British industry. The higher taxes affect consumer demand, and reduce the funds available for investment already limited by the uncertainty generated by the threat of expropriation. At this stage the resulting economic crises begin to become obvious, and the programme is put into cold storage, and divisions begin to appear within the party. The popularity of the party falls into decline. By-elections are lost. A general election follows. Eventually the party is defeated. A Conservative Government is elected and the scene is then set for the second half of the cycle, represented by the Labour Party in opposition.

When elected, the Conservative Government sets out with a good will to remedy the situation with which it has been left. Like every other administration, for the first two years it is to some extent dogged by the consequences of the policies of the previous administration. These have not yet worked themselves out, and the new policies are seemingly ineffective. Because financial realism is almost always unpopular, the party begins to lose support. By-elections are lost. Back benchers become restive, and, at this stage, most Conservative administrations begin to lose their nerve and relax their policies before they have had time to take effect. In the meantime the trade unions use their industrial muscle to force up wages, and they are, of course, vigorously supported by the entire Labour opposition in the House of Commons. So far as industrial pressure by the unions consists in demanding a share of profits actually made this, of course, would be arguably beneficial, though it would not improve the chances of investment. More often it is a threat of inflicting losses on businesses not particularly thriving. In extreme cases, as in February 1974, the threat is a threat to deprive the population of the necessary means of carrying on its life. This has become increasingly easy, partly as the result of technological developments in the actual processes of production, partly as the result of secondary action undertaken by unions in support of one another, and partly as the result of nationalization in the public sector, and amalgamations in the private sector. Apart from the obvious constitutional objections to this, if the pressure succeeds, as happened in February 1974, and the government is overthrown, the successor government is put in a position when it can only yield to current and future threats. In February 1974 the result was that the rate of inflation, which was then at an intolerable 10%, rose immediately and increased rapidly up to 30%. If the pressure does not succeed, as in 1926, the hardships which follow are held the responsibility of the government, and a general election follows at which it is defeated. In either event the cycle is now complete, and the stage is set for another Labour Government with another programme involving another burst of current expenditure, another round of borrowing, another economic crisis, and a further turn in the downward spiral of British economic hopes and British influence in the world.

I have hitherto been treating the progress as cyclical. But at this stage I must draw attention to a process which is linear and irreversible. This is the so-called ratchet effect of socialism. Labour manifestos always contain a so-called shopping list, based on Clause 4, of industries due, to adopt the euphemistic jargon, to be taken into public ownership. If they have proved unprofitable, the argument is presented that they have failed the nation under private ownership. If they appear profitable, the argument is that the profits should accrue to the public and not go into the pockets of individuals. If they are sufficiently large it is urged that they must be captured in order to possess the commanding heights of the economy. All these arguments are hypocritical because the fact is that, under Clause 4 of its constitution, the Labour Party is bound to take into common ownership *all* the means of production, distribution and exchange, whether they are successful or not, and, to a considerable extent, whether the units concerned are large or small.

But the point is that the process is inherently irreversible. This, of course, would not matter if public ownership were demonstrated as the more or an equally efficient method of production. But, in practice, this has not proved to be the case. The unwieldy monopolies which have emerged have not been particularly well run, have not commanded the services of managers or chairmen with the genius to manage huge enterprises of this size, have proved particularly vulnerable to trade union or government pressure, and unable to generate adequate investment from their own surpluses, which, incidentally, have not usually existed. Worst of all, the workers in them have lost the sense of loyalty to the enterprise which, for instance, characterized the old railway companies. In exchange, the expropriated shareholders have been given negotiable paper in place of fixed assets, commanding a fixed rate of interest payable for the most part out of the public purse. If losses are made, the public has thus to pay the double burden of compensation and subsidy.

But the principal point I am making is that the process is irreversible. Successive Conservative Governments have considered the possibility of denationalizing these units, but have succeeded only in breaking off a few pieces. The remaining bulk has proved in practice as ugly and as indestructible as the Admiralty fortress at the end of the Mall.

Of course, the long-term effects are not simply economic. They are constitutional and social. If tyranny consists in the concentration of power, freedom consists in its diffusion, and this involves a policy of breaking up concentrations in the centre, decentralizing into smaller units. Can it really be satisfactory that the head offices of our railways, our mines, our steel, our post office, are concentrated in one place? And can it be satisfactory that that place should be London? Is it altogether surprising that the Scots, the Welsh and occasionally others wish to break away from the centre? But what would they be able to take with them? And are there not other and better methods of decentralization?

As I have said, there was a time when I had hoped that the two processes I have described would come to an end, and that we should, in due course, come back to a two-party system, which did not involve the dismal downward spiral involved in the first, or the linear ratchet effect involved in the second. While Hugh Gaitskell was leader of the Labour Party there was hope that the Labour Party would follow his evolutionary and pragmatic radicalism. But Hugh Gaitskell was first repudiated, and later died. There was another period, during the Chancellorship of Roy Jenkins, when a period of economic orthodoxy seemed to be about to make the Labour Party a credible master of our finances. Unhappily this resulted in a higher figure for unemployment than was acceptable to the unions. In 1970 when a Conservative administration sought to reflate gently, the unemployment showed itself more resistant to treatment than had been hoped. The Conservatives then began once more to lose their nerve and reflated more vigorously. The result was that trade union wage demands became more difficult to resist. The events of the autumn of 1973 then began to unfold, and in 1974 the Labour Party returned to power once again pledged to overspending, unable to resist union demands, and with Denis Healey and not Roy Jenkins at the Exchequer. So far from abating, the vicious cycle was repeating itself more viciously than before, and the linear ratchet was given two or three more strokes of unprecedented length.

The result of this has been the position in which we now find ourselves. Year after year, the borrowing requirement has continued, each borrowing adding to the national indebtedness, and an increasing fraction of each borrowing being devoted to servicing the existing debt, thus being absolutely unproductive. Within weeks, rather than months, inflation rose from 10% (already intolerable) to 30%, and despite the so-called social contract, itself inflationary, has never returned to its former level. Even if it had, the pound sterling would have sunk to a new low level from which there is no reason to believe it would ever recover, with the prospect of it sinking to a lower level still, equally irreversible, since the lower level of inflation would still be inflationary. National independence, which depends as much on financial stability as on military invulnerability, is a thing of the past. The most that can be achieved, or is being achieved by the new loans and facilities, is to hold the pound at its new low level until consumer expenditure, public and private, brings it to a lower level still. Of course, all this is written from the point of view of a Conservative. But the point to which it brings me is the same as the point to which his reasoning, starting from entirely different premises, has led Mr Benn. The existing system has failed. We cannot go on as we are. We have a choice to make, and one option is that we proceed, as he wishes to do, to a full-blooded socialism. I believe this would involve a siege economy, at

least for a time. I also believe, although I expect Mr Benn
would dispute this, that this alternative is wholly inconsistent
with the continuance of any form of Parliamentary democracy, if only because, though there are in fact more compelling reasons, no party government could pursue
consistently the policy required for a period long enough to
survive successive general elections and pendulum swings.
In my view at least, a more authoritarian regime than we
now possess would be needed, with all that that implies in
the field of restrictions on personal freedoms and fundamental rights.

But is the alternative to this dismal prospect a continuance of capitalism? To this question I propose two
answers. In the first place capitalism is itself a word invented
about the age of Marx to describe something which has never
existed as a system and certainly does not exist now. Whatever may have been true in 1848, the date of the Communist
manifesto, the control of industry has passed very largely
from the individual owner to that complex institution, the
joint stock company, in theory controlled by its shareholders,
who are many, but, in practice, largely by its directors, whose
main virtue is, of course, not purity of morals or disinterested-
ness, but that they operate independently of government,
and therefore create a greater diffusion of power. Being
not so vulnerable to purely political decisions, they are not
so destructive of economic efficiency. If what this country
needs is greater economic efficiency more power should be
given to their elbow.

I believe these arguments to be conclusive, but whether
they are conclusive or not, what I am trying to say is that
our economic system has evolved continuously, is evolving
and, left reasonably alone, will continue to evolve. It never
could be described by a single label, and, given another
twenty-five or fifty years of continuous development in a
free society, could not be labelled then by any description
which would fit it now. The choice is not between socialism
and capitalism, but between an open and evolving free
society with limited government, and a closed society
dominated by ideology and controlled by a dictatorship, even
if one that is based on election. Given this choice I am not in
doubt which way my fellow countrymen would choose to go.

My second answer is more pragmatic, and more parti-cularly directed to our present situation. The dominant factor in our present condition is our poor performance compared with our principal competitors in Europe, America and Japan. What needs to be done is to identify the factors which have made them succeed and us fail. Whatever else may be true of all of them, our successful competitors are all operating under what Mr Benn would call the capitalist system. Whilst he and I agree that some-thing in our present method of operation has gone wrong in order to account for our recurrent failure, it cannot be that element in our present arrangements which he designates as capitalism. I shall in fact be arguing later that if that element had been given greater freedom from government inter-ference we should have fared better. I shall also be arguing that part at least of our failure has been due to the lamentable trend to centralization and over-government which has dominated our thinking since the war, and not only in the political field. From that point of view, smaller tends to be more beautiful, but for the moment I am content to rest on my belief that, whatever else has been the cause of our failure, it is not capitalism, or free enterprise in any form. What Mr Benn has to explain is not only our failure, but our free competitors' success.

I cannot pass from this subject without making one further point. There is a certain strand of opinion which is prepared to say that no radical change is required in our present method of carrying on because everything will be all right when our North Sea oil wells come into full pro-duction. This I believe to be the most dangerous heresy of all.

I do not at present complain of the economic assumptions upon which the heresy depends. I am prepared to assume that the oil will last longer than at present is thought likely, that the low-cost producers will not decide to undercut us, that, before the oil runs out, other sources of power, equally helpful to our competitive position in the world, may become available to us. I am also prepared to assume in our favour that no other external or disruptive forces interfere with our free exploitation of the off-shore fields. But even so, if I am right in ascribing our failure to compete as due to internal weaknesses in our national arrangements and social and political outlook, these will continue to operate to our detriment whatever addition to our national resources may be found or maintained. Indeed, the possession of oil as a new natural resource may prove as demoralizing to us, and in the end as disastrous, as the possession of the South American gold and silver mines to royal Spain, that it will provide an excuse for not putting things right, for allowing ideological considerations to prevail over practical and objective argument, for continuing to persecute the middle class, overtax the enterprising, discourage thrift, and feather-bed the unions and factory workers. If so, the possession of oil will be a curse rather than a blessing. A decaying society cannot achieve salvation by the possession of a new natural resource, especially when based on an extractive industry. It needs to identify and remedy the causes of its decline. We shall not cease to live in the City of Destruction whilst we still possess within it the seeds of our own failure to compete.

VIII

THE PRESSURE GROUP AND THE UNION

In the classical model of Parliamentary government, the sovereign people exercises its authority through the ballot box by electing representatives to a legislature exercising plenary powers and giving effect to the will of the people after debate.

In fact, of course, what actually happens has never borne more than a superficial resemblance to this model. To give coherence to the choice of the people and to give consistency to the policy of the government parties are required and dominate the scene both inside Parliament and at election time. It has always been my opinion, at least until recently, that the ideal number of parties is two, on the lines evolved in many Anglo-Saxon countries, the reason being that, if there is a multiplicity, none of them commanding a majority, the tendency is for the real wishes of the people to be left behind. To create any kind of stable administration an accommodation is necessary, and this can only be the product of bargaining between party groups inside the legislature. The result, so I have always thought, is a weak and unstable coalition for whose compromise policies the electorate has never voted, and never would have voted if they had been given the choice. It is for this reason that I have never so far given my full support to various schemes of proportional representation. The idea that the legislature should be a mirror image of the votes cast as the result of the inconsistent wishes of an electorate divided into many groups seems to me to offer a sure guarantee that no coherent national policy will ever be evolved, and no issues squarely faced. Least of all is it likely to provide assurance that the dominant will of the electorate will be carried out. Until recently at any rate, I had rather see the executive govern-ment reflect the coherent attitudes of the largest organized minority, even if I had doubts whether the whole legislature should be composed on the same lines. I will return to this theme when I consider the function and role of a second chamber, and the conception, almost peculiar to Britain, that a legislature should be accorded unlimited powers to alter the laws of the land.

In the meantime, in the last chapter I observed in a rather restricted context that in recent years the system I have hitherto supported has broken down. It has produced a sort of see-saw motion in policy, a polarization rather than a continuous evolutionary development, and, as the result of what I have described as the ratchet effect, a movement of national policy which is both linear, irreversible, and probably entirely against the determined wishes of a large majority of the electorate. When they thought they were voting in favour of a relaxation of controls, which they regarded as too rigid, and a more generous measure of expenditure on the needs of those whom they regarded as badly off, the electors found themselves committed to a programme of nationalization and expropriation which they neither desired nor thought in their own interests. They were caught in the manifesto and mandate trap, which compels them to accept all or nothing in a party's platform.

There is, however, another feature of democratic life which is directly due to the dominance of two great national parties. This is the pressure group. Since all great national parties, while pretending to be monolithic, are in fact coalitions agreed only about a few great issues of public policy, there are a large number of questions demanding attention which they are very reluctant to handle at all. Moreover the very pressure on Parliamentary time imposed by the overcentralization of our government means that a ready excuse can be found for ignoring such questions, or shelving them by one device or another. In addition to these matters there are a vast number of other causes which enlist the enthusiasm of minorities. These are driven to organize themselves in one way or another to bring pressure on Members of Parliament and candidates, local authorites, party organizations, and when they do not get a hearing, or even when they do not get their whole way, they adopt various means of making themselves a nuisance until they get it. Unfortunately there is a noticeable tendency for them to succeed in inverse proportion to the legitimacy of their methods. At the far end are the extremists carrying guns; at the near end are the occupiers or diggers-up of cricket pitches either to secure particular aims such as the release of a particular prisoner, or more general political objectives like the prevention of a visit by a South African team of players, or the use of the Welsh language on road signs or in court. In between are all kinds of demonstration, legitimate and illegitimate, violent and peaceful, noisy or silent, each demanding attention for a particular cause in which the public as such are usually profoundly uninterested and which can sometimes be shown to be wholly unreasonable. It is difficult to believe that this is a rational way of carrying on debate. If it is the price we pay for freedom, it may be that it is often worth paying, though, by the time that it degenerates into active terrorism as with the PLO and the IRA, and their various splinter groups and fringe organizations, one is quite sure that the price is altogether too high, and that freedom itself is threatened by yielding to it.

However this may be, there are two factors in the increase in numbers and range of the pressure groups which are surely obvious. The first is that, quite irrespective of merits, the growth of pressure groups reflects a loss of confidence in the Parliamentary machine to produce results in consequence of national Parliamentary debate without pressure beyond that which is generated by the inherent strength and reasonableness of the case. The clear indication is that the case will be ignored altogether unless it is shouted or chanted in the form of a slogan or, worse still, brought to the attention of an indifferent Parliament by direct interference with the needs or pleasures of the public. Government, it is thought, has become too remote to listen at all. Either it is too preoccupied with matters either trivial or irrelevant to the wishes of those who sent them there, or it is too divided to produce a rational or coherent policy at all. So the enthusiasts resort to pressure, and then to demonstration, and finally, perhaps, to illegality and, in a few cases, violence.

But the second point is that if campaigns conducted on these lines succeed, as they often do, their success does little to reduce this impression. Whistling to keep their courage up, the government may pretend that what has happened is a victory for common sense. At the bottom of their hearts they know that it is nothing of the kind. What has happened is that they did not yield to reasonable argument, and, when they did yield, they were made to do so by pressure, or even worse. The moral is easily learned. If you want to get your own way, you must make a nuisance of yourself, and what matters is not the strength or reason of your case, but the amount of nuisance you can cause. Such a principle is not necessarily immoral. But it is inherently amoral and its social and political consequences may be serious. Power tends to move away from an inarticulate majority in favour of various articulate and more or less militant minorities. The remedy must be in some ways to make government better able to represent the majority, and in other ways to make it less remote.

When the pressure group represents large numbers of extremely militant people possessed of actual power, the results can be more serious. They can be catastrophic. This is what leads me to discuss the role of the unions in recent controversy. In this country unions are quite differently organized and pursue quite different methods to unions elsewhere in the free world. So far as violence and corruption are concerned, I am quite persuaded that they are infinitely superior to the unions in America which, however much they may have benefited the wage earner, have rather a terrifying history of bloodshed and graft behind them. As compared with the continent of Europe, British unions are far less apt to be Communist led or controlled. But they are far more monopolistic than either their American or European counterparts. They are split into far more numerous exclusive units each protected from competition by the Bridlington agreement, which, if it were made between employers, would be immediately struck down as contrary to public policy. Each union pursues the interests of its own members almost implacably even where to do so ruins the plant in which they work, or throws members of other unions out of work. Whatever their faults, American unions tend to go in for long-term agreements, and, on the whole, to observe them. European and American unions are far less resistant to technological change, and being far more based on a particular industry or plant, far less prone to demarcation disputes, quarrels amongst themselves, and unofficial strikes.

It is, however, when they enter the pressure group business with the government that the British unions are seen at their worst, and, in my view that most serious constitutional development of which they have been guilty is the so-called social contract for which so much has been claimed. It is obviously right for any government to keep in constant touch with unions and management regarding the industrial and economic policy they should pursue. Unions and management are deeply interested in the movement of wages and prices, the tax burden, the level of employment and industrial training and safety, to name only a few subjects, and both sides can only gain from a free and continuous exchange of wisdom. It is also clear that both sides in industry may have important views on social benefits. But this is not the implication between versions of the so-called social contract. Rightly or wrongly, successive governments have believed that wage claims in excess of what is reasonable are among the causes, and possibly the decisive cause, of inflation. This may be right or wrong. Excessive wage claims may be to the advantage of the wage earners as a whole or they may not. If they are, the unions can hardly be blamed for pressing them. But a good many people are satisfied they are not. It is obvious that one person's wage claim is another person's price rise, or perhaps everybody's price rise. It is less obvious, but none the less true, that one person's wage claim, if granted, throws another person out of work. It is also true that it leads, other things being equal, to an adverse move in the balance of payments. A total wage policy is therefore something, at least, as likely to be in the interest of the workers as the Bridlington agreement, and there is much to be said for a policy of wage restraint agreed on by the unions and presided over by the TUC. But what it certainly is not is a bargaining counter to be traded for slabs of public policy between the TUC and the government. Either the public policy traded away is in the public interest, or it is contrary to the public interest. If it is not in the public interest it should not be pursued even if nothing is offered in return.

If it is in the public interest it should be pursued even if something very attractive is offered for giving it away. The government has no mandate to trade away public interests as part of a bargain with sectional interests, and it may be added that sectional interests can have no mandate from their members to trade away their legitimate interests in return for slabs of public policy. A contract in this sense is a double abomination. It sacrifices the interests of the public to a section of the public, and it involves both an assumption of power by the leaders of that section which is not warranted by any democratic principle, and a disregard by both sides of those whose interests are not represented. In the recent instance these may amount to more than half the nation. If trade unions wish to forswear wage restraint they are entitled to say that it is in the interest of their members to do so. But in assessing that interest they are not entitled to treat as matters of private negotiation between themselves and the government any fiscal or monetary measures taken by the Cabinet in order to counteract the damaging effects on the general public of what the unions have been doing. The possibility of such counter-measures is itself a factor which the unions must take into account in assessing the interest of their members.

The effects of the social contract were in fact extremely damaging. Designers, self-employed professional men, managers, various types of public servant and producers of food were all extremely hard hit. Some have been going abroad. Others have been alienated, possibly permanently. When one reflects on the organic connection between trade unions and the Labour movement, one is bound to conclude that contracts of this kind cannot be allowed to be repeated without permanent harm to a democratic constitution.

But the ultimate condemnation of the abuse of union power is that they have collectively betrayed their own membership. Wages, which started lower on the continent, are now higher than in Britain whether measured in absolute terms or in relation to prices. In Germany they are something like double. Powerful trade union officials attempt to blame this on the lack of investment, or the quality of management. But when managers are not given long-term stability and are penalized personally by taxation, when profits are condemned, when prices are controlled and no funds are available for capital expansion, and when confidence is absent how can legitimate complaint be made of the absence of investment or the quality of the managers who remain at home? By selfish, short-sighted and narrow-minded policies, the unions have thus betrayed their membership, their country and their class, and the workers in foreign industries, better led than ours, have reaped the benefit.

IX

THE DANGER OF TAKEOVER

I have been discussing our system of government on its merits. I have tried to show that it is breaking down. It accords unlimited power to a legislature normally dominated by a party, and within that party by the leadership. It is elected by a method which ensures that the majority in the House is always more or less unrepresentative of the electorate. It has been shown quite clearly in practice that even a relatively small majority can use its inherent advantages in such a way as to carry through legislation for which the electorate would never have given approval, and that the power of dissolution gives even such an administration a better than even chance of perpetuating its life.

I have not mentioned hitherto the greatest danger of all, remote no doubt, but still present as a possibility, easily preventable at present, but, if it were ever realized, almost impossible to counter without violence.

This is the danger of takeover, that the whole system could be infiltrated from without and made the vehicle of a real tyranny committed to the destruction of the present order of society. Clearly if, for any reason, the system ceased to be operated in good faith such a position could be reached. Party caucuses could be infiltrated and could select candidates for safe seats committed to extreme courses and pledged, implicitly or expressly, to obey orders from outside. Trade union elections, at which only about a twentieth part of the rank and file can be induced to vote, could be manipulated, even without the actual rigging which has undoubtedly taken place from time to time. Once the union is represented by extremists the whole immense card vote of the entire membership can be thrown into the scales at trade union, or party, conferences. At the local level, industrial disputes can be fostered, or allowed to fester. At a general election, fiercely fought and producing a narrow majority, the

Parliamentary party can be threatened or cajoled to carry out an extreme programme, written into the manifesto by executive or conference decisions decided by the organized minority. Economic crisis can be made a plausible excuse for draconian measures forced through Parliament by the three-line whip and the guillotine, and the House of Lords swept on one side, even if by that time it has not been abolished. The monarchy, effective as a guarantee against illegal takeovers, would then merely be a helpless instrument in the hands of government, and, if it were not, could be abolished. Once in the hands of an unscrupulous party the whole machinery of the constitution could be harnessed to the purposes of the power in order to effect irreversible change. This was clearly realized before the war not only by Sir Oswald Mosley but even by such respectable characters as Sir Stafford Cripps and Clement Attlee, both of whom threatened to govern by decree under emergency powers. It is quite clear from the latest documents issued by the Communist Party that this is not far from their present strategy and thoughts and even this manifesto is considered too mawkish and weak by the breakaway wing. It was in this fashion that Allende ruined Chile to the point at which a military takeover by his opponents became possible, and became itself the parent of evils the full extent of which have not even yet run their course.

The danger is, as I have said, remote. Under Mr Callaghan it is reasonable to hope that moderates in the Labour Party will recover their confidence and their ascendancy. But it is obvious that the National Front or the left wing of the Labour Party would be compelled to govern by the methods of dictatorship if either ever obtained power. Happily, National Front opposition to the Conservative Party is open and not by way of infiltration, and in any event we are less open to infiltration from the right than is the Labour Party from the left.

But we should be crazy, should we not, if we failed to place legal and constitutional barriers against such a danger, if, for other reasons, the changes involved were shown to be either harmless or desirable? If it is shown the powers of central government are excessive and ought to be diminished or devolved, if for general reasons there ought to be a Bill of

Rights entrenching at least the provisions of the European Convention, if it is established that our present system of voting is open to criticism, and its dangerous results uncontrolled by any effective second chamber, then surely we should be spurred to take action now, when the result would be to render impossible an assumption of power by infiltration and takeover which all would resist if it were made openly?

I do not claim the danger of takeover as my main reason for urging constitutional change. To do so would be absurd, though the danger is not so remote as to be altogether negligible. What I do say is that the reforms which I have to urge on other grounds would make dictatorship by takeover impossible unless backed by an immense majority of public opinion. Of course, if backed by an immense majority of public opinion, dictatorship would be unavoidable by any means. But we should at least deserve our fate if we failed to take steps to prevent a takeover by anything short of this.

What are these steps? The first steps are clearly outside the scope of the present discussion. They include an adequate system of defence, and an adequate police force to keep civil order. No legal, and few political, systems are proof against takeover by force, like the establishment by Hitler of the Quisling regime in Norway, or the destruction by Cromwell of the Rump of the Long Parliament in England. National independence requires the ability and will of a nation to defend itself against all comers, and side by side with an adequate defence system, must be ranked a system of alliances sufficient to overcome any potential adversaries. If the smaller Western democracies had realized this before the Second World War, and had been willing in place of neutrality to ally their fortunes with Britain and France, it is even possible that war could have been prevented. Instead, Norway, Denmark, Holland, Belgium, Luxembourg, Finland, Estonia, Latvia, and Lithuania, fell victims to takeover from without, and Ireland, Switzerland and Sweden only survived because we did not lose the war. Alliances and defence systems are not just right-wing inventions designed to divert resources from the social services and distract attention from the need for socialism. They are the necessary guarantees of the integrity of any state against capture of its political apparatus by external force. When the political apparatus consists of an omnipotent Parliament virtually consisting of a single chamber, dominated by a vastly powerful executive, and controlling a centralized bureaucracy, and completely uncontrolled by an effective judicial machinery, the danger must, at least in theory, be regarded as all the more real.

Equally important as a guarantee against takeover is financial and economic independence. No bankrupt can be free to live his own life, and so long as we continue to borrow we shall continue to be subject to the pressures of our creditors. But in this too I would be straying beyond the limits I have set myself if I were to pursue the matter in detail.

Wholly within the limits I have set, however, are the types of safeguard to which I look. These are of three kinds. The first is legal. There should be limits set beyond which politicians may not be allowed to go without a special mandate protected by proportional voting and referenda. These limits should broadly follow the restraints demanded of government by any constitutional Western state, and must be policed by the courts through an adequate legal procedure.

The second type of safeguard would so rearrange the balance of forces within the separate organs of the constitution as to make dominance by any one of them impossible. The identification of these will involve an examination of the possibilities of a reformed second chamber, and devolution of power to broad regional assemblies. The third type would consist in an attempt to increase the extent to which the people itself is now able to involve itself in the electoral process without impinging on the coherence of policy and the effectiveness of decision making. Clearly this part of the enquiry involves an examination of existing voting processes and the value, if any, of referenda on particular issues.

The total package demands a re-examination of the totality of our constitutional arrangements. Taken in isolation I do not treat the danger of takeover in the strict sense as among the major problems facing us today, except in the sense in which I have shown that Labour Governments are intrinsically in the hands of union leadership and committed to policies which they endeavour to carry through against the will of the electorate. But the possibility of takeover must be seen in the context of the far more dangerous drift of ideas working in conjunction with the insensible dynamism of existing attitudes towards a state of elective dictatorship. The remedies I prescribe against takeover, are, therefore, basically the same as those which would be effective against the less dramatic but more real and insidious danger of existing tendencies extrapolated into the not so distant future.

X

SMALL IS BEAUTIFUL

Ever since the war the work of centralization has gone on apace. It has not been confined to the work of government, or even the public sector in industry. For most of my life at any rate I have been content to accept the trend as beneficial, or, at worst, as inevitable. In recent years I have come to question the assumptions on which it is based, and to regard it as, at least in part, responsible for the alienation of the people from government, some of the symptoms of which I have been examining. When I speak of the alienation of the people from government I do not only mean from Parliament and politicians, I include the alienation of the workers in the public sector of industry from the national boards. I include, of course, the pressure groups and demonstrations against particular government decisions, or the separatist movements in Scotland and Wales. But I mean even more than that. I make the same judgement of the alienation of the workers from management in British Leyland or Fords as I would of the miners from the Coal Board, the Scottish Nationalists from Westminster, the CND from official defence policy, or the demonstrators against Maplin, or the proposed coal mines in Belvoir Vale. All are symptomatic of a disintegrating society that has lost confidence in leadership, the City of Destruction in which we are living.

I do not wish to be wholly dogmatic about this. There are technological processes which involve large units. It is not as a rule sensible to try to build a small electrical generating station, or a minute petrochemical plant or steel works. There is a minimum and a maximum level for all types of activity, and probably an optimum level somewhere in between. Nevertheless you do not tend to find damaging strikes on a national scale in industries which are split up into small units. Alienation begins to appear in all large conglomerates of human beings which are run from the centre. Some form of devolution, federalism, call it what you will, seems to be necessary in all branches of human activity. There is depersonalization in all large-scale human activities for which a heavy price in terms of human relationships has to be paid.

The arguments in favour of centralization are extremely convincing. When I first went to the Admiralty we were already in the process of amalgamating the three service departments into a single Ministry of Defence. This process was completed under Peter Thorneycroft, and the old offices of First Lord of the Admiralty, and the Secretaries for War and Air were down-graded to minor ministerial appointments. I well remember the arguments in favour of the change, almost universally accepted, then and now. There would, so it was said, be greater unity of control and the end of inter-service rivalry. Vast economies would be effected by common services and procurement, and further savings in expenditure by the reduction in central staffs. Above all, in place of divergent counsels there would be coherent and unified advice from the chiefs of staff. I can recall how disappointed I was when I discovered that the new Ministry of Defence would cost more and not less and employ more and not fewer people. We were told that this was inevitable, at least at first. The process of working out the changes would inevitably involve additional recruitment. Soon there were other disappointments, and the promised economies never arrived. In fact, of course, the economies have largely been made in the field of fighting power and equipment. We spend six thousand million pounds a year on defence, and in relation to other nations we have the smallest forces we have ever possessed. Even the promised unanimity of advice has proved a delusion. In place of the arguments, bitterly fought, and tenaciously debated by and in front of ministers, an ominous silence prevails. There is a sort of military Butskellism, a compromise which satisfies no one and represents no coherent thinking at all.

Then I was a member of the government which sanctioned Sir Keith Joseph's *gleichschaltung* of the Hospital Service. As a result, the old teaching hospitals lost their independence, and a very great deal of the voluntary work by medical experts which goes with independence has disappeared. Instead a new class of medical administrator has emerged, serving large area boards, and commanding what in this country passes for an adequate salary. But where is the morale, dedicated service and *esprit de corps*, which characterized the old Middlesex, Guy's, St Thomas's or even Elizabeth Garrett Anderson? Once more, the faceless men have taken over. All administration develops into bureaucracy. Human relations are depersonalized and men begin to think of themselves as numbers. But the expense of running an efficient bureaucracy is much higher than that of running a voluntary organization.

When British Leyland emerged from BMC and Leyland hopes were high. At last we were going to have a unit of sufficient scale to challenge the American giants. But what, in fact, have we got, but a twentieth-century dinosaur with vast immobile limbs and a tiny head? I hate to refer to the nationalized industries, lest I be thought guilty of a primitive obsession against public enterprise. But have we had the managers of a calibre to infuse any national corporation with the enthusiasm or efficiency we were promised in the early days of nationalization? Can such men be found? Granted that the old mine owners were hard men, and their memory bitter. Is Hobart House much more popular in the coal fields? Certainly British Rail hardly inspires the loyalty of the old Great Western, and the Gas Corporation has been much more prone to disputes than the old Gas Companies. The former electricity grid which enabled co-ordinated supply to take place under a system of separately run power stations certainly never threatened a national power shut-down. Have we never studied the problem of the optimum size for different types of human activity? It is clear enough that the old Britain, dominated as it no doubt was by grandees, landlords, and millionaires supported by parsons and squires commanded a good deal more effective loyalty and enthusiasm than any so-called democracy based on full-time MPs, huge metropolitan districts, and a swollen Civil Service. May it not be that nations can be held together more effectively by personal relationships, mutual respect, and small units working independently of one another than by vast combines, professional headquarter staffs, institutions centralized in the capital or even in provincial capitals? Perhaps we would do better to break things down rather than continue to build them up into soulless amalgamations dominated by men who become faceless in proportion as they are not personally known.

The trend towards centralization is not limited to the fields which I have so far attempted to describe. It covers the whole field of administration, public and private, though it is with the public with which I am principally concerned. Take, for instance, the field of education. I quite understand that the all-age village school had to go. A few survived until my own first period of office in 1957, and, as they gradually dropped away, letters would appear in the press, local and national, bemoaning their demise. I knew we had to part with them, but I recognized all the same that with them part of the traditional soul had passed out of village life and out of education too. We had lost something of value, and though what we had put in its place was more efficient and, I believe, made better standards possible, at the elementary stage we had removed the child further from the home, made parental influence more remote and school more impersonal.

But what are we to say of the new comprehensives? In precisely those areas where the young feel alienated from society great school businesses are being set up, with literally thousands of pupils differing widely in ability, inclination, and outlook. The Butler Education Act spoke of a comprehensive *system* of education. It said nothing of a comprehensive *school*. What do we think we are doing with the young people we seek to 'educate' in this way? A school is a community, and an eleven-year-old is flung into a community of thousands, where to his timid eyes he appears to count for practically nothing. The best of the old grammar schools and secondary modern schools may have had their faults. But they ran out at manageable figures, and, though most of them were built at a time when school design was far less imaginative than it is now, the new comprehensives are now housed in the very same buildings sometimes three-quarters of a mile apart brigaded together into a 'comprehensive', as I believe, just because for the time being parents, unaccustomed in their youth to secondary education of any kind, liked the sound of something which did not run the risk of their children being subjected to a test in which they might fail. Too late now, it is coming to be realized that the new comprehensives are altogether too big. The average child is being deprived of an opportunity to shine in a community in which he could excel. The gifted child is deprived of the education to which he is entitled, and the stimulating association with those of equal talent. Compounding their folly, our educationists now are beginning to send off those who survive the system at all into sixth-form colleges, thus depriving the sixth-form pupils of their moment of responsibility, and the school community itself of its natural leadership.

I begin to wonder too whether the system of local government inaugurated whilst I was Lord Chancellor is all that was promised. I quite understand that the old division between boroughs and counties was for many purposes obsolete and inefficient. But some of the boroughs had regalia dating back to King John, and the counties even earlier to Anglo-Saxon England and the Danelaw. They provided our county regiments and found our cricket teams, recalled our civil wars, enlisted in our political battles. Could none of it be kept? Will we ever feel for Avon or for one of the Metropolitan Districts what we felt about Sussex or Somerset, or Bristol, or Oxford, or King's Lynn? Something went out of English life when Peter Walker started to implement John Redcliffe Maud. Could not some of it have been saved? Is it not possible to recreate some of it now?

Our government has always been more centralized than most in Europe except, perhaps, in metropolitan France after the revolution. We have gained greatly by its strength. But what was tolerable when the functions of government were few and its powers limited, has become the strangling Whitehall bureaucracy we know today. And we gain nothing by 'decentralizing' motor licences to Swansea, or the Welfare State computer to Newcastle-on-Tyne. We have not really decentralized anything by so doing. We have only moved part of the central bureaucracy away from London, not always improving its efficiency thereby, but never creating a renewed local patriotism, a closer communication between the individual and the people who govern him.

When I went up to the North-East of England in 1963,

there were, so far as I remember, 146 local authorities of various kinds, and within this immense and variegated structure there were special purpose committees of various sorts each communicating with a different government department in London. The local education committee communicated with the Ministry of Education, then in Curzon Street, the housing committees with the Ministry of Housing, the road committees with Transport and so on. But there was no central meeting place in Newcastle or Durham for them all. For, so far as I know, the first time since the Doomsday Book I brought up the representatives of the different ministries to make a coherent plan and to leave an ongoing presence in Newcastle which I hope still, at least to some degree, continues. My ambition was to hand over the whole apparatus to some locally elected regional Parliament. But that is just as far from fulfilment then as now.

I sometimes get letters asking why, when we all of us fought so well and side by side in the war, there is so much class distinction in industry and commerce, and such polarity between management and workers. Sometimes foreign industrialists with British branches or subsidiaries come here and lecture us. Some blame management for their treatment of the workers. Some blame the unions, their archaic structure, and their proliferated numbers. I am inclined to think that there are indeed organizational problems, which to say the least partly explain the malady.

When I was a platoon commander in the Rifle Brigade, I commanded a body of men not more than twenty-five in number, and in the exigencies of service, usually a few less. But to these twenty-five men there was one officer (me), one platoon sergeant, and at least three corporals or lance corporals. There is nothing like this structure in industry. We were a motor battalion and cooked by sections, usually very nastily, in the desert. But the unit was small. We lived, we slept, we worked, we fought, and when on the move we largely ate together. There was hardly a cross word between us, and when I was on my own on the move the men in my HQ truck saw that I never lacked for a cup of tea when they brewed up one for themselves. There was no district secretary of a trade union to get between us, with a national organization to back him up. There was no poaching nor any arguments about who does what, though naturally enough there were individual skills. It is not for me to tell industry, especially large-scale industry, how to manage its affairs. But I like small units when everyone knows everyone else and, yes, loves them too, and I do not fail to note that whereas the job and the conditions depend on the plant, be it large or small, the unions are based on the area and the craft.

At all events I feel sure that, up to a point at least, small is beautiful. Where things must be big let them be subdivided. And let loyalty be to the working group whatever that may be, and let the large organizations devolve their central bureaucracies.

XI

PERMISSIVENESS

It is both difficult and dangerous to dogmatize about the standards of legal or moral behaviour effectively observed in any previous age. We are apt nowadays to suppose that the Victorian age was a period of prudishness and puritanism, of law and decency, of Christianity and order compared with the present, and that the Edwardian age which followed it until the beginning of the First World War was, even if we admit that it was vulgar and raffish, one in which the vulgarity and the raffishness had not penetrated deeply enough in society to destroy the underlying patriotism and national unity inherent in the British people.

Like most other generally held opinions, these superficial judgements probably contain more truth than falsehood. But the case on the other side is formidable. One does not have to dig very deep in Victorian literature, or in one's own family memories and traditions to realize that respectability was only skin deep. No one, for instance, who is familiar with Trollope's novels can fail to see that the crust was very thin indeed, and that underneath was a seedy world of dishonesty, violence, and vice. If one looks at Dickens, the contemporary *Punches* with their barefoot street urchins, or the Gladstone diaries, or the accounts of my own grandfather encountering the waifs and strays of Victorian London in his ragged school, one realizes that law and order, and the rules of respectable conduct, even amongst women, were not at all as they are portrayed in the popular legend. Edwardian society was not merely raffish and vulgar at the top. It was riven by class hatred, industrial strife, political acrimony, and the stirrings of a new age which, had it not come to the surface naturally in the agonized aftermath of the First World War, might well have burst forth in civil conflict and even revolution. One simply does not know how to generalize accurately about such matters.

Nevertheless, popularly received opinions do have a certain value as such, and probably reflect the totality of an actual state of affairs as seen through the socially coloured spectacles of the literate and articulate. Such a view may be biased but it is at least an observation of actuality. Ages of violence, and great wars, do have a disintegrating effect on social and ethical values, and on artistic standards and political regimes. No one who has studied Greek art and literature before, during, and after the great Peloponnesian war can doubt that. The Weimar Republic was quite different from the Imperial regime which preceded it and from the Hitler regime which destroyed it. The Third Republic in France was indeed the weak and corrupt thing it was portrayed. The French Revolution and the Directorate were different in morals and ethics from either the *ancien régime* or the First Empire. In each case the catalyst was war and, in some of the instances, defeat. The post-Vietnam atmosphere in the USA, the post-Suez atmosphere in Britain are other cases in point. I am not at the moment arguing the rightness or wrongness of the moral issues involved. I am not at present seeking to choose between Roy Jenkins and Mrs Whitehouse. There is a good deal more to be said for each than the other would allow. I am simply saying that if in fact one wishes to identify the moral symptoms of a disintegrating society, one can do worse than examine what was said and written, before, during and after each major cataclysm of which we have records, including the present. My candidates for examination would be the Athens of 450–350 BC, the last days of the Roman Republic and early days of the empire, say from 100 BC to 50 AD, the history of France, say from the death of Louis XIV to 1820, the history of Germany from 1870–1970, and the history of Britain from 1912 to 1977. In each case, there is a loss of belief in the standards of a regime which has suffered defeat or decline, a growing cult of anarchy and sexual indulgence, an openness about criminal behaviour and a disposition to defend it, a proliferation of strange and inconsistent ideologies and beliefs, a refusal to accept that there is a standard or norm to which human behaviour and the sanctions of human laws should approximate. In each case there is a breakdown in family and marital relationships, a weakening of parental authority, an assault on the authority of the state and existing institutions marked by a series of more or less febrile and unsuccessful endeavours to re-establish that authority, and various attempts, none permanently successful, to establish an authoritarian regime. Finally, after the whole landscape has been altered, some sort of pragmatic compromise is reached in which a new society can grow up with new systems of comparative authority established. There is, I believe, an established connection between sexual permissiveness and violence, between crime and political instability, between the commercial exploitation of the less controllable instincts of mankind and social and revolutionary change, between the discrediting of religious experience and vice and human unhappiness. The difficulty seems to me to reside in discerning which element in the syndrome of symptoms I have been trying to describe is causative and which is purely the effect of underlying causes of a different kind. The truth is that probably each inter-acts on the other. But I remain of the opinion that to some extent at least the whole syndrome starts with political instability, based on the inability of existing institutions to cope successfully with a challenge brought about either by an external threat, or by some new factor within society which, for one reason or another, is not given adequate recognition.

Since I am not writing this book primarily about external affairs, I do not propose to explore the theory, which I none the less believe to be true, that many of our present evils stem from the too rapid disintegration of the British Empire brought about by the joint action and policies of our American friends and allies, and our Communist adversaries, and their failure or refusal, based on the incompatibility of their ultimate aims, to place anything as stable in its place. What I am, however, anxious to do is to point out that, however much in the past our social instability can be said to be due to the insufficient regard paid by existing institutions to the interest of the industrial worker, the balance has now swung entirely the other way. The organized working class serving in large-scale industry and represented by the trade unions has so much power economically and industrially, and so little understanding of the real requirements, economic, social and political of the various other elements in society that the balance needs urgently to be redressed.

More than almost anything else we need urgently an element of restraint and limitation deliberately structured into our political machine in the interests of minorities, the nationally conscious Scots and Welsh, and Irish, the alienated middle class, the self-employed, the scholar, the religious community. I do not believe that this can be done without a radical overhaul in our political arrangements. We are suffering from the basic paradox of all unstable societies, an excess of authority coupled with an insufficiency of stability and order. We must curb authority with constitutional limitations. We must increase order by the protection of individual and minority rights. There must be less government. But what there is must be better obeyed, and, I hope, better loved.

XII

ELITISM AND DEMOCRACY

Britain has lost her pre-eminent position in the world. What then is her role? What goals can we pursue if we are denied the position of power from which in the past we have achieved so much? There comes back to my mind the haunting phrase of Milton:

> Let not England forget her precedence of teaching nations how to live.

This seems an arrogant phrase in the second half of the twentieth century. So I will substitute another which equally means what I am trying to express. I am trying to preach the pursuit of excellence as the key to national recovery. I mean this prescription at every level, material no less than political, moral and social.

In material terms it means that we must go back to the time when 'British made' or 'Made in England' was a guarantee of quality, when an Englishman's word was his bond, when British Justice was such a sure guarantee of fair play and dispatch that merchants from all over the world stipulated English law as that governing their arrangements and English Courts and English judges the arbiters of their disputes. We must go back to the day when London was a synonym for financial integrity and commercial efficiency, and we could rely on the quality of craftsmanship and the acceptance of the binding character of promises whether legally enforceable or not.

I believe it can be seen that there is no other salvation for British industry. We are among the oldest of industrial countries. Our original sources of prosperity, coal, textiles, steel, shipbuilding, are either being taken over by developing countries, or yielding before newer and more sophisticated methods of achieving the same purposes. With India and Pakistan, with China, Singapore, and Hong Kong, and above all with Japan as industrial rivals producing cheap goods, well serviced, of high quality, with an adequate supply of spare parts, after sales service, and reliable dates of delivery we simply cannot afford not to be perfectionists, not to be seeking constantly new fields of endeavour. This does not mean of course that we must confine ourselves to the top end of the market, and produce only luxury goods as infinitely durable and as exorbitantly expensive as Rolls-Royce cars. Nothing has been more depressing than our being driven out of one mass market after another, by the superior excellence of the foreign product, the Honda moped, for instance, over the Raleigh runabout, or our failure to make well-engineered standard articles in preference to the exotic, the unusual, or the frivolously extravagant. Excellence can be achieved in anything you undertake. The product of the mass market is as capable of excellence in its own way as the article of luxury, custom built.

But, of course, the quality of goods in industry, the excellence of their design, the standards of industrial management, the skills of salesmanship form only one facet, and probably one of the least important, of the matter which I am putting forward. In every field of endeavour success depends on excellence, and excellence is most successfully pursued in the company of others following the same objective. Education, training, inspection, discipline are the necessary conditions of successful achievement. It may or may not have been a waste of effort to put men on the moon. But when they got there, and the result was broadcast live from our satellite, every carefully rehearsed movement, every elaborate procedure designed to counter unforeseen mishaps eloquently displayed the necessity for a conscious perfectionism if excellence is to be achieved. It was as true in ancient times as it is now, in the erection of the Taj Mahal as in nuclear engineering, in the weaving of a carpet from Isfahan as in the printed electronic circuit of a computer, in the perfectionism of the Brigade of Guards or the crew of a submarine, in the penmanship of a miniature Koran, or a work of art, a poem, or piece of music.

Whatever can be said against them this is a truth apparently fully realized on the other side of the Iron Curtain.

There is nowhere where greater emphasis is laid on the need to identify talent, to train it, to reward achievement, or to praise examples of collective endeavour or individual leadership.

Can we say the same of ourselves? Hitherto, I have been comparing two sorts of democracy, the democracy of elective dictatorship and the democracy of limited government, greatly to the advantage of limited government as being the more efficient, the more admirable, and the more just. But it is just possible that in one vital respect we may get the worst of both worlds.

The evil doctrine has been spread that all forms of distinction are somehow undemocratic, and that all forms of collective or individual excellence are somehow immoral. The word used to mislead us, and to corrupt us, is elitism; and what I am preaching as the condition of our survival will inevitably be condemned on many lips as elitist.

I am not ashamed to admit the charge. In the days when Britain was truly a nation we were a people of relatively small communities, almost all in their different ways avowedly elitist, competing for excellence with rivals similarly dedicated to excellence, boroughs, counties, crafts, sports, professions, services, railways, industries, each thinking itself the best of its kind, all aiming at something slightly different, all, like my own profession of the Bar, at once highly competitive and generously friendly, and all agreeing that, whatever internal differences there might be, British was undoubtedly best.

Was all this wrong? My answer is an unequivocal 'no'. Elites of all kinds are among the conditions of success for a modern nation, particularly a democracy, and, amongst all democracies, particularly for Britain which has lost her empire and found no new role. Elitism and democracy are compatible and complementary; elitism and democracy serve each the cause of the other, democracy generating and fostering the different forms of elite, the elite serving and vitalizing the democracy by preserving its dynamism and combating its tendency to philistinism.

An easy, but fatally superficial reply is the facile answer that all depends on education. If all were educated up to an adequate standard, it is argued, there would be no need of an elite. But it is precisely the advance of education which creates the need. When I was Minister in 1957 two young anti-elitists wrote to me that it was useless for them to study mathematics any more as they knew they were approaching what they described as the push-button age. Since they did not sign their names I was unable to reply that it was precisely the approach of the push-button age which created the need for more, and better mathematicians. The further education is taken, the more various the specializations which it develops, the higher the standards it achieves, the more the gifted child or young adult begins to realize his true potentiality in life and leisure, in work and recreation, the greater the diversity between each and all, and the greater the difference in achievement between the best and the worst. So education does not solve the problem. In a sense it creates it. So long as culture was for the very few and the very many were preoccupied with the struggle for survival the problem of elitism did not exist. In the dark ages the elite were almost eliminated. So far as they continued to exist at all they were driven into monasteries and forbidden to breed, like Abelard and Eloise. The only elite which remained at large was a military caste, mounted on horseback and encased in a heavy defensive armour. In modern democracies, and particularly perhaps in Britain, the elite are encouraged, almost cajoled into existence, but when they begin to show their colours and display their talents they tend to be rejected.

If I am correct what British democracy should fear is not elitism, but philistinism, by which I mean the persecution of talented minorities, and the pretence that goes with it that their values and standards are simply expressions of subjective opinion, and probably of less importance than the views of the largest minority of uninformed opinion as represented by a public opinion poll, or perhaps the result of a general election.

It may seem at first sight that my fears are fanciful, or, at worst, exaggerated. How, it may be asked, can you persecute minorities when they hold almost every position of responsibility in the state? What are the elite? They are the heads of government departments, judges, religious leaders, captains of industry, leaders of the professions.

They are the establishment. How can they be members of any persecuted minority? It is the inarticulate multitude, it will be said, the industrial workers, the peasants, the common man, the housewife, who need protection. They are the exploited, and the very minorities for whom I appear to be so anxious are, it will be argued, either themselves the exploiters or at best indifferent to the exploitation. Such at least is the attitude adopted by the articulate and intelligent Communist authors of 'The British Road to Socialism', and many others on the left.

But consider for a moment. All men admire certain types of perfection in others. Beauty in a woman, strength of body in a man, are considered on all hands matter for congratulation, even flattery. But suppose that it be said of a child, of a woman, or a man, that he is clever, does not a note of criticism, of warning, even of downright depreciation creep into the voice? Other things being equal, the British, or at least the English, are inclined to suppose that a clever man is less honest and less sensible than a stupid one. My own experience leads me, on the contrary, to believe that almost the opposite is nearer the truth. But, alas, this does seem to correspond with the voices I hear on every hand. 'I am only a simple man.' 'Of course I do not understand the niceties of your argument, but this is how it would appear to the man in the street.' Brains are not of course by themselves either a guarantee of virtue or even a hallmark of common sense. But, by and large, clever men usually learn, sometimes by the hard way, the wisdom of being as good as they are capable of making themselves, and acquiring the practical skills necessary to their success.

I do not wish to keep harping on the question of education. But there is one point of importance to emphasize here. It is very generally accepted, and rightly, that children who have special handicaps of mind and body need special provision, in the ordinary school whenever possible, but at special schools or at special times when necessary. But does it not also follow that the same may be true of the specially gifted child, or at least some specially gifted children? The potential world-class athlete, like Evonne Goolagong, or the potential ballerina, needs to be spotted early and given proper training from the start. But there are intellectual and artistic athletes as well as physical. Would it not be strange if these too had not special needs, if they were not resentful and frustrated at deliberate neglect of their potential talents? May it not be dangerous to humiliate them or slight them, or worse still, make them think that the gifts of which they cannot fail to be conscious are not appreciated and can find no place in the community to which their loyalty is owed? Is it a coincidence that revolt amongst the young appears to be commonest where the talented most obviously congregate? May it not, in addition to the perennial struggle of youth against age, be at least in part a revolt of talent against the mediocrity and philistinism of current opinion?

What are the functions of an elite? The first, as it comes to me, is the cultivation of genius and originality in conditions most favourable to achieve the advances necessary to human progress. Ask oneself any question one chooses about the significant figures in human history. Examine the history of world religions, Christianity, the Hebrew prophets, Muhammad, Buddha. Seek for the initiators of scientific advance, Newton, Einstein, Galileo, Copernicus, Faraday. Examine the influence of Shakespeare in English, or Cicero in Roman literature. Consider the great political leaders, or the great technologists like Brunel. In each case, at the base of a new discovery or a new movement you find a man of intellect and originality, often unpopular and persecuted in his lifetime, but able to gather round himself and convince a segment of opinion sufficient to perpetuate his work and finally overcome resistance in the light of his genius. Democracies, like other societies, neglect such men at their peril.

Apart from the men of genius, there is the specialized circle of informed opinion, which can engender the atmosphere within which genius can flourish and its products be discussed and to whose informed judgement the man of genius can appeal. There must be established authority in matters of taste, intellectual perception in matters of aesthetic judgement or informed opinion. Though Jack be as good as his master in this world, or the next, it is simply not true that the truth or falsehood of subtle questions can be settled by counting heads or appealing to the result of an opinion poll.

But thirdly, elites are of many kinds. They are not limited to the egg heads or the intellectual or artistic giants or even to the heroes of the various sporting fraternities. In a free society they are as numerous as the activities which are at once its characteristic, its glory, and part of its justification. Anyone who seeks excellence can join an elite of some sort in a democracy, and, in a democracy in which uniformity is not the aim, and diversity is encouraged, each man and woman is free to join a restricted group in which he can excel and offer service. Such groups are not class conscious examples of social or intellectual or aesthetic snobbery. They are the salt of the earth. They are the church workers, the youth leaders, the club secretaries, the trade union officials, the welfare officers, the pigeon fanciers, the Scouters, the allotment holders, the members of residents' associations, the Salvation Army Captains, the exponents of almost every free activity you choose to mention, that is except the things which mean drabness, boredom, cynicism, non-involvement in society, and mediocrity in all things. So in my democracy let elitism in all its multiplicity flourish. It is the leaven in the lump, the salt in the dish, the thing without which life is flat, stale and unprofitable. It is the pursuit of excellence in all its forms. Without it we shall not be able to escape from the City of Destruction.

XIII

IN PRAISE OF LAW

The four central ideas upon which a government of the Western type may be said to rest are law, liberty, representative government, and an impartial administration of justice. Of these law is the first in time to be established, and the framework within which the others can live, move, and have their being.

The enforcement of law rests, of course, upon those possessing political power, and since the possession of political power cannot self-evidently be said to be based on moral right, this has given rise throughout the ages to legal positivism in one of its many forms, the simplest expressed of which is that of Austin, that law is nothing else but the command of the ruler. In a sense all lawyers must be legal positivists. They could not advise their clients if they did not take political authority as a given fact and argue their cases before the established courts without questioning the basis upon which they were established. Political authority in the modern world is almost always based historically upon some forcible acquisition of power, and since it is in the nature of sovereignty to demand a monopoly of force, even the most primitive of sovereigns is faced with the necessity of settling disputes, enforcing the settlements, and imposing penalties on those who take the law into their own hands. The moment, however, that this happens the ruler is faced with the problem of deciding on what principles disputes are to be settled or penalties imposed, and, if only because there is no other body of doctrine available, he finds he must settle them on the basis of existing custom, or, if he wishes to alter the custom, of some general set of ideas which he outlines himself. In practice, therefore, while law must always be ascertained by a formal enquiry as to the rules recognized for the time being by the sovereign power, the actual content of legal rules is always governed by reference to principles which claim to owe their reasonableness to something other than an arbitrary exercise of will. At first, of course, these principles are thought to be immutable, but as, gradually, it comes to be recognized that no principles are wide enough, or clear enough, to be applicable to every case, and no society stable enough to be able to endure for long under an unchanging set of rules, organs of legislation need to be evolved. The moment it comes to be seen that a mere appeal to tradition is not good enough, the search begins for a principle of jurisprudence which will give a clue to the making of laws as well as to their enforcement. In the eighteenth century, when the old Common Law was creaking and grinding to a halt, Bentham, who was Austin's close friend, provided such a principle in the form of utilitarianism, the greatest happiness, as he formulated it, of the greatest number. Legal positivism and utilitarianism reformulated so as to meet various obvious objections have ever since provided what has recently been described as the ruling theory of English writers on jurisprudence.

But the law as it exists, and as it is applied, is radically inconsistent with either theory. Those crazy fellows, the judges, and that even more crazy institution, the House of Commons, have never acted as if the theory of legal positivism were true. The poor dupes are sadly under the impression that law as it exists, and still more as it ought to exist, has something to do with morality and justice. Only that superb legal positivist, Adolf Hitler, was content to adopt the true Austinian theory that law is what the Führer chooses to treat as law. Every formulation of legal positivism, however sophisticated, breaks down at this precise point, unless all that is meant by the theory is that law means, and means only, the result which will come down from the judges if a disputed question is referred to the courts. This is a perfectly sensible stance for a practising lawyer to take, provided, but only provided, that he is aware of, and sensitive to, the arguments which will persuade the judges to reach that result, and those arguments are always connected with the popular conceptions of justice and right.

Equally, although the general welfare, which is how the theory of Bentham is now more usually formulated, sounds all right as a principle for legislation until you analyse it, utilitarianism, however carefully defined, runs clean counter to the universal conscience of mankind. Individuals and minorities have, so we poor fools are convinced, rights and interests on which they are entitled to insist even at the expense of the general welfare or the total apparatus of the modern state claiming to represent it. Of course the theory can be restated so as to assert that those interests and rights are in truth the most enlightened form of the general welfare. But this supposed restatement destroys the theory of utilitarianism, and does not restate it. Of course this line of reasoning is not generally recognized beyond the Iron Curtain, or even, say, in Uganda. Nevertheless we who live in the outer darkness of Christianity and liberal democracy still cling pathetically to its truth. Though he little knew it, Bentham, no less than Austin, was providing the intellectual framework for the concentration camp and the gas chamber as much for the policies which inspired the Manchester school economists or the social democratic wing of the Labour Party. Stalin and Hitler are among their spiritual descendants no less than Herbert Spencer or Roy Jenkins. It is strange that two such orthodox children of the enlightenment, and the long line of civilized disciples which has followed their teaching to become the ruling theorists of jurisprudence should have failed so completely to understand the logical consequences of their line of thought. Law is not the creature they suppose it to be, and, if it were, the rest of us would fearlessly refuse to recognize it as law.

For the central question both for jurisprudence and for political theory is this. Law is about compulsion. Government is about compulsion, the coercion of men and women to do what would otherwise never have been their choice. What earthly justification has one man to compel another in this way simply because he is entitled to put on a red gown or wear a wig, or because after his name he writes the mystical letters MP, or before it the equally mystical 'Right Honourable'? 'None at all', says the anarchist, and, of course, on his assumptions he is right. 'He needs none', says the determinist, and, of course, on his assumptions he too is right. Of course if you believe that man is only a trousered ape, or no better than a social insect, living only for the benefit of his termitary or hive, no kind of moral question can arise. But then jurisprudence is reduced to the level of a practical hand book for training ponies or retrievers, or keeping bees from swarming. But training for what? And who is the bee keeper? And why should bees not swarm? And as for ants or termites, why not put them down altogether as garden pests? To this the proponent of determinism can provide no rational answer. After all, he is at the best only another trousered ape if he is right, or perhaps another worker bee in the hive.

But lawyers and lawgivers, judges and voters, do in fact appeal to a theory to which they choose to give the high-sounding names of justice and morality, right and wrong, responsibilities, duties and moral rights, to which, it will be remembered, Bentham gave the splendidly derisive label 'nonsense on stilts'. Rousseau, of course, evaded the central difficulty by inventing a contract. Men were bound to observe their civic obligations because of a primeval agreement between noble savages. But there never was such an agreement, and, if there had been, the descendants of the parties could not be bound. The fact is, they are so bound, but not so slavishly or absolutely that they are obliged to honour the decrees of a tyrant. However difficult it may be to formulate the connection, there is a relationship between morality and law, between justice and reason, without which all forms of government become a tyranny, and all their subjects slaves.

In the end, no system of jurisprudence can stand comparison with the actual facts of forensic practice, or the demands of the human conscience if it does not assert a system of natural rights and natural justice of some kind, and this involves exploring the metaphysical riddle of free will, and the enigmas of moral responsibility and value judgements of right and wrong. The writer on jurisprudence or political theory or the statesman who ducks this issue is building an elaborate mansion on foundations of sand. This remains true of all systems of government, the anonymous majority which rules a Parliamentary democracy not less than the most explicit dictator of them all. The moment democracy ceases to pay attention to the limitations and restraints which all governments must observe, it ceases to be a form of free government and becomes an organ of tyranny. This is the central argument of this book. It is failure to recognize this cardinal fact which marks the essential difference between the two theories of democracy of which we must choose one and reject the other.

XIV

IN PRAISE OF FREEDOM

Of all the emotive words which stir the hearts of men, freedom is amongst the most powerful and, at the same time, amongst the most elusive. It is easy to see what freedom means to a chattel slave, an oppressed subject nation, or someone in prison or one of the labour camps of the Iron Curtain countries. It is less easy to define its meaning in, say, medieval France, or eighteenth-century England.

I am not inclined to pursue the sophistry which was so popular just after the war, of saying that political freedom is useless without economic freedom, or that, before the war, to the working class, freedom meant freedom to join the dole queue. Obviously poverty, like illness, ignorance, or mental or physical handicap, reduces the value of freedom in the sense in which it is understood in the West, by constricting the number of valid options open to a man. But affluence is no substitute for freedom, and, in terms of practical politics, affluence has not often been attained or permanently kept except as its accompaniment.

Nor do I wish to pursue in this context, what is less of a sophistry, but something of a red herring, the familiar distinction between liberty and licence, freedom and permissiveness, independence and anarchy. Elsewhere I must, of course, insist that liberty and law, freedom and law abidingness are not enemies, but companions, two of the co-ordinates which alone can build a society into a coherent and stable picture. Freedom, like law, postulates a human race which is capable of free will and responsible choice. It cannot be imagined in a community of animals or insects. It is no inhabitant of the wolf pack or the termitary. It is one of the ideas which imply inevitably the making of value judgements, the acceptance of personal moral restraints based on some ideas of right and wrong and not merely on matters of subjective personal preference.

But freedom in the sense in which I am now discussing the

word does imply an absence of external personal restraints deriving from the will of others, be they individuals, governments, or organizations. It is a word which describes the area in which personal choice can operate untrammelled by the personal choices of others, circumscribed though the area may be by impersonal external factors like the weather or geographical location, or the absence of economic or physical or mental resources. Most of us understand what we mean by freedom in this sense, though many of us may find it difficult to define or explain philosophically.

Attempts have been made from time to time to define freedom in terms of 'freedoms', 'liberties', or 'rights', and no doubt these definitions have practical value, whether contained in the Atlantic Charter, or the Declaration of Human Rights of 1948, or the European Convention on Human Rights, or the first few amendments to the constitution of the United States, collectively known to Americans as the Bill of Rights. But I do not intend to explore this fairly well-mapped territory here. Whatever attempts are made to define 'freedoms' or 'rights', the exceptions which have to be recognized to give adequate protection to the state in times of crisis or war are so numerous, and themselves so inexact as to make it possible for an unscrupulous government to ride roughshod over individuals and minorities, especially when the government is backed by an excited or alarmed public opinion, and supported by powerful and disciplined armed forces and police.

I simply wish to make two or three quite separate points about the philosophy of freedom in its political sense, which we ignore at our peril. If I am correct in believing that only a plural society can effectively command patriotism, and that only a society which respects the rights of individuals and minorities can justly be called free, or even just, there are consequences which have to be faced.

The first is that the only freedom which counts is the freedom to do what some other people think to be wrong. There is no point in demanding freedom to do that which all will applaud. All the so-called liberties or rights are things which have to be asserted against others who claim that if such things are to be allowed their own rights are infringed or their own liberties threatened. This is always true, even when we speak of the freedom to worship, of the right of free speech or association, or of public assembly. If we are to allow freedoms at all there will constantly be complaints that either the liberty itself or the way in which it is exercised is being abused, and, if it is a genuine freedom, these complaints will often be justified. There is no way of having a free society in which there is not abuse. Abuse is the very hallmark of liberty. Except in a society of saints, if there is no visible abuse, you may be sure that in practice there is no freedom.

The second point is that if there is to be a free society there must be the maximum tolerable division of political power. It is a cliché that all power tends to corrupt, and absolute power corrupts absolutely. It does not matter how far this is true or not. There is no such thing as absolute power in human society. But it is clear that to the extent that power is concentrated there is no freedom. This is why democratic states, particularly those influenced by the Anglo-Saxon tradition, have always demanded a division of power, sometimes defining basic rights, sometimes dividing authority by federation, sometimes concentrating on the separation of the executive from the legislature, or the independence of the judiciary, sometimes creating legal safeguards, and sometimes creating political checks and balances, such as a voting system designed to prevent the domination of any of the organs of government by a single political element.

The third and the most important point, however, is the dynamic role which freedom has played in the last three or four hundred years in the progress of the human race in every sphere. There have been eras in human history when everything seemed to stand still for centuries, even, perhaps, for millennia. If some ancient Rip Van Winkle had gone to sleep in Upper Egypt in the age when the Pyramids were being built at Mena, and had woken up about four thousand years later, say on the eve of Alexander's conquests, I dare say he would have been more impressed by the resemblances than the differences. The same gods were being worshipped. The same hieroglyphs appeared in the temples. The same agriculture, based on the same divisions of the land and the same old Nile flood, was being practised. The same types of Pharaoh wearing the same symbols of monarchy ruled the land. The military art was not much different. The nations of the known world seemed to change only in the sense that the more they changed the less essential difference there would appear to be. Vanity of vanities, the awakened sleeper might have murmured, there is nothing new under the sun. There are similar points to be made about China, and to some extent about India, and the pre-Columbian civilizations of Latin America.

But compare the present age with the past three hundred years. A civilized English landowner in the eighteenth century could no doubt look back to the age of late Republican or early Imperial Rome with a certain sense of recognition. But in truth he was living in an age of gradually accelerating change. Ever since the invention of the compass, and the ocean going sailing ship, and the cannon and musket, still more since the invention of the steam engine, and the internal combustion engine, and the harnessing of electricity, the world has been changing at an exponentially increasing speed.

Nor has the change been limited to technology. Never since the age of Pericles or that of Cicero has the ferment in the hearts of the human race been more active. The change has been seen in religion, politics, art, music, the literature of all languages, philosophy, leisure. There is no branch of human activity which has not been affected.

Now what is the cause of all this? One part of the answer, I believe, is freedom. Freedom has certainly accompanied these changes, and the changes have been accompanied by demands for still further liberties and rights. Obviously changes of this order give rise to tensions and conflicts, spiritual, political, social. But unless we are prepared to say that they are bad, or unless we are prepared to say that the association with freedom is purely coincidental, then we restrict or abolish freedom only at our peril.

We can now claim a certain amount of empirical evidence to support our contention. It is more than sixty years since the Russian Revolution. One state after another in the East has adopted a system the opposite of freedom. If the socialist contention were correct, sixty years is quite long enough to begin to show results. But what results does the Russian Revolution show, and what results are shown in the other Iron Curtain countries? In the West, we have to restrict immigration. But there it requires walls, machine-guns, state trials and a Gulag archipelago to keep in place the inmates of the workers' paradise, where the proletariat is alleged to exercise a dictatorship but where, in fact, government of the people is exercised by the party on behalf of the system. There are no consumer goods in the shops of a range, in quantities, or at prices comparable with the West. There is a shortage of agricultural produce to such an extent that one of the largest agricultural areas of the world had to import grain from capitalist North America, and butter from the surplus of industrialized Europe. In socialist countries there is perpetually a bad harvest. Their main exports to the Third World are sub-machine-guns, and sophisticated weapons of destruction. Even their science, where it is not consciously orientated to military purposes, is largely derivative from that of the free world.

It is no good the Communists pointing to the remaining poverty in the West until they can show that the prophecy of Marx is coming true. But it is not coming true. For the last century or more the poor have been becoming richer, and in western Europe, the rich have been becoming poorer in actual living standards. It is freedom which has created this great advance, and, where freedom has been curtailed the advance has not taken place.

This brings me back to the City of Destruction in which we live now. For here freedom is being curtailed again. We, who were pioneers of it, are now throwing it away, and, as we throw it away in handfuls, so our progress is being curtailed, so our talented spirits are beginning to leave, so our standard of life, our morals, our law abidingness, our national solidarity, our very respect for our political institutions are beginning to decline. It is worth while asking how this process can be reversed. Because, while freedom is among the exceptional states of men, tyranny is the norm, and, whilst freedom can give way to tyranny by easy stages, freedom can only be won at the expense of tyranny by prolonged agony, violence, and martyrdom. When we are

97

told that the alternative to our present situation is socialism, we may do well to remember that freedom is the mother of plenty and progress in things spiritual as well as material, and enquire whether socialism here or elsewhere is compatible with either.

XV

IN PRAISE OF REPRESENTATIVE GOVERNMENT

At the date of its destruction the walls of Pompeii were covered with election posters. As is well known the generals in ancient Athens and the Consuls in ancient Rome were chosen by election. But these were elections to a particular office, like the election of the French or American Presidents. None were elections for a representative government like the elections to the British House of Commons. In his will, the Emperor Augustus discloses that at one time he had contemplated the election to the Roman Senate by the municipalities of Italy. But in the ancient world the idea never came to anything. The idea of representative government in the modern sense was specifically an English invention, and, from England, it has spread throughout the globe. Its object is to prevent the oppression of the mass of the people by arbitrary rule. Though its logical conclusion is universal adult suffrage, it developed slowly and reached its end only within our own lifetime. As every schoolboy knows if he has studied Burke's letter to his constituents, representative government is not at all the same thing as representation by delegates obliged to obey the mandate of electors. A Member of Parliament should follow his conscience and should not be coerced by external pressure, either from pressure groups, or his local constituency association or even his own party whips. We all know that the reality is rather different. But this should not lead us to forget the theory in its orthodox purity. Although decisions are taken collectively by simple majority vote, they ought to be taken after debate, and the individual votes, when they are cast, influenced by argument.

Of course total independence in a Member of Parliament is in practice, and, I would have thought in theory also, an impossibility. 'Madam,' the 14th Earl of Derby is alleged to have said to Queen Victoria, 'an independent Member of Parliament is a Member of Parliament who cannot be depended upon.' There was more than mere cynicism in his observation. Policy is a coherent whole. If you put up the Old Age Pension or the pay of the armed services, you may not be able to reduce the income tax, or increase the building of hospitals, schools, or prisons. You may not logically vote for all three, although you may logically oppose all three. Aneurin Bevan once said in my hearing that priorities are the religion of socialism. Like most epigrams, this was inaccurate. All policy, like all design, is an attempt to combine divergent and sometimes inconsistent requirements. When the recipe is decided upon, the quantity of each ingredient diminishes or increases the quantity permissible of the others. This is not so much the religion of socialism as, to borrow a phrase from Harold Laski, the grammar of politics.

The actual volume of work required of a modern member drastically reduces the number of subjects on which he can speak, or even on which he can express a worth-while opinion. It does not excuse him from voting, because if he limited his votes to those subjects on which he is a master, the resulting policy would be a lottery depending on which members of which parties studied what. The result of course is party organization and party politics. 'Gentlemen,' said Disraeli, 'Parliamentary government is party government. You cannot have one without the other.'

This is why, throughout my life, I have sought to remain a loyal member of one of the two great parties in the state, and why, in doing so, I have not regarded myself as in the least false to my own sense of personal independence, integrity, or to personal patriotism or devotion either to the well-being of the nation at large, or the interests of my own constituency. I still believe that representative government based on universal franchise, with the necessary background of political parties, each with its party loyalty and discipline, is part of the essential structure of a free society.

But I now wish to point out some qualifications. Should the government also be Members of Parliament or should they have a separate mandate? In Britain we regard it as axiomatic that they should be members of one of the two Houses. In the United States it is regarded as equally obvious that they should not. This is because they believe in separation of powers in government into three distinct parts, the executive, the legislature, and the judiciary. We believe it to be essential that the executive government should be Members of Parliament belonging to a party capable of commanding a majority in the House of Commons. The American constitution places it in the hands of a President separately elected. Neither theory is morally reprehensible. Each has worked well over a long period of years. In fact, the American is rather closer to the original division of power in the British constitution than our own present practice. Originally it was the business of the King to choose his ministers and govern according to his conscience, as the American President does to this day, and the business of Parliament to pass changes in the law (then thought of as exceptional) and raise the money, as the Congress does to this day. But, in twentieth-century Britain, the two functions of legislature and executive government are inseparably intertwined. Part of the present malaise in the country is, I am sure, due to the fact that the public is uneasily aware that you cannot appeal effectively from the legislative proposals of a government to the majority in the House of Commons. In other words, where government tends to be arbitrary under our system, the people's will is not adequately protected by its representatives in Parliament.

Granted that the functions of an individual member are too complicated to enable him to decide each question separately on its merits, what powers should collectively be placed in the hands of the sovereign body? In Britain, in consequence of the fact that, traditionally, Parliament was the trusted defender of liberty against the executive, no limits were placed on its powers. So far as law making is concerned, Parliament is omnipotent, and since the government can normally rely on a majority in the Commons, and the House of Lords is virtually impotent when it comes to a dispute, there are few effective limits to the powers of a government in a position to legislate unless a minority of government supporters is prepared to vote with the opposition. Practically no other civilized country has invested its representatives with such unlimited authority. Almost all, like the United States, have owed their independence or freedom to successful revolution or voluntary cession, and in almost every case have chosen to limit the legislative powers of their parliamentary assemblies. All have been prepared to cede to their courts the right to enforce minimum safeguards to minorities or individuals.

Granted that Members of Parliament, and therefore governments, are invested in Britain with the almost divine attribute of theoretical omnipotence, one would surely suppose that particular care would be taken to see that they are properly representative and carefully selected. We all know that this is far from the case. We are careful to see that the House of Lords is not elective at all, and therefore wholly unrepresentative in the strict sense of anything, except, where it is so, of personal distinction. Our House of Commons is elected on the first past the post system, of all systems of voting the most likely to produce domination by an organized minority. Our candidates are chosen by committees of selection wide open to infiltration by extreme, or, occasionally, even corrupt elements. The idea that our system is one of representative government is therefore one which requires considerable qualification. According to one story, which he is said personally to have repudiated, the late Archbishop Temple is alleged to have told a gathering of students: 'I believe in one holy Catholic and apostolic Church, and I very much regret that it does not exist.' Whilst, therefore, I am prepared to praise representative government without qualification, I am not prepared to say that our own is fully representative.

Quite apart from this, whilst representative government may hope to defend the majority or mass of the people against arbitrary government by a minority, even a genuinely representative system cannot by itself protect minorities or individuals against arbitrary government by the majority. Under our own system of voting no one can protect individuals or other minorities even against the largest organized minority. These disadvantages are diminished where there is a plurality of parties, each one of which has some chance of winning some elections or some divisions in the House. But this is not always so, at least in some areas in the United Kingdom, and then one-party government, with all its vicious tendencies, sets in. As has been seen in some areas of north-east England, Derbyshire and Wales, when whole areas are held as party fiefs, tyranny and corruption can not be far away. One-party government can defeat both the theory and practice of representative institutions.

The conclusion is that, even where plurality of parties is possible, representative government cannot adequately defend individual or minority groups which are not in a position to enforce their will. For this purpose it is necessary to reinforce individuals and minorities with legal rights enforceable in the courts which cannot be removed at the whim of a majority of the legislature. This conclusion has been almost universally accepted abroad. But it is no part of the constitution of the United Kingdom. Unless all these safeguards exist, the mere provision of representative institutions may be a dangerous illusion giving a false sense of security against arbitrary rule.

XVI

IN PRAISE OF JUSTICE

Of the four pillars of freedom, law, liberty, representative government and an impartial administration of justice, I treat the last as bearing the same relation to law as representative government bears to liberty. Law represents the system of rules to be applied to the settlement of disputes between individuals and government, or between individuals and individuals. Justice, in the sense in which I am using the word in this context, is the means of ensuring that the rules are applied correctly and impartially. No doubt the original laws in force in a country at any given moment of time owe their origin to custom or past legislation. It is the business of representative government, executive and legislative, to formulate new rules or to maintain old ones. But it is the business of the courts to see that they are applied properly to existing disputes when they arise. This involves an independent judiciary, a fair procedure and a reasonable access to the courts on matters which are properly justiciable.

Here we come to a most important point. Everyone has heard of Magna Carta. Every schoolboy learns of the victory of Parliament over the Stuart Kings. But only a minority have been sufficiently well trained to realize that quite as important a landmark in the history of Britain was reached when Parliament insisted that judges could only be dismissed for misconduct, and did not hold their office at the sovereign's pleasure. The independence of the judiciary from the government is every bit as fundamental to the maintenance of a free society enjoying liberty under law as is representative government or a multiplicity of political parties, or the correct formulation of rules governing the relations between government and individuals, or between one individual and another.

Today this independence is more necessary than ever. The area of political control is constantly being extended. Each extension involves an increased risk of abuse of power by those who have achieved it. When the main danger to the independence of judges lay in the possibility of their arbitrary dismissal by a monarch, it was possible to think that making their dismissal possible only on resolutions by both Houses of Parliament would provide an adequate safeguard of their independence. Clearly now it is not. One of our two Houses of Parliament, the House of Lords, is constantly threatened with abolition whenever it challenges even the most absurd aberrations of the other, while the other House is more and more unrepresentative in character, more and more intrusive into fields which it previously never ventured to enter, more and more dominated by ideology, and more and more in the hands of party whips controlled by government and motivated by partisan considerations.

Direct attacks on the judiciary, almost unknown when I entered Parliament forty years ago, rare even ten years ago, are now constantly being made, not merely by back benchers, but by ministers, and indirect and snide references to them are habitually promoted from behind the ramparts of a few academic institutions, and even on the radio and television. These animadversions naturally provoke popular manifestations of hysteria whenever judicial decisions prove unpopular or are thought too lenient or too severe.

Obviously all judges are not equally wise, and obviously some judges make remarks which, although reasonable enough in the context of a particular case, are, when reported out of context, manifestly unsustainable. But judicial courage, previously required only when the judge was risking possible offence to an individual monarch or his favourites, is more and more required when he is inadequately protected by the government, assailed by back benchers and even ministers, and criticized by name in the press or in the media. Is it surprising in these circumstances that, surrounded by these reputedly respectable examples, unsuccessful litigants should show decreasing respect for orders by the courts? Never since the latter part of the seventeenth century was it more important that the independence of the judiciary should be safeguarded by express rules embodied in the law, and safeguarded from intrusion by the legislature as well as the executive.

Of course, the possibility of their actual dismissal, and

even their prospects of retarded promotion (a far more real peril) are the least part of the problem. The more important necessity is that justiciable issues should be left to the courts and not dealt with by the executive or Parliament, and that what is left to the courts, however politically sensitive, should be genuinely justiciable, that is, dependent on the genuine ascertainment of facts, or upon the strict application of a clearly formulated rule of law, and not dependent on the subjective opinions of the individual judge.

By some academic writers the idea is being sedulously fostered that, in arriving at their decisions, judges are influenced by social class and political prejudice. This can only be believed by dedicated Marxists who genuinely consider that anyone who does not consistently promote socialist principles is *ipso facto* a Tory or a class enemy. This view is as self-revealing as the words of the man in the story who said to his friend: 'You must be drunk. You have two noses.' Of course the judges are children of their time. It is useless to expect twenty-first-century opinions from twentieth-century men and women, and if by some exercise of clairvoyance judges were so far in advance of their time, their views would not be acceptable to their contemporaries. But the possible range of options open to a judge in any given case is extremely narrow – far narrower in most respects than that available to judges on the continent of Europe or America. A judge in Britain is hedged about by a far more restrictive view of precedent than are they, and, since most decisions nowadays consist in the interpretation and application of Acts of Parliament, it is even more important that the rules for construing Acts of Parliament followed by English and Scottish judges are far more rigid and limiting than in any country in the world not operating the British system. In addition, our traditional method of Parliamentary draftsmanship is so much more detailed than in any European country as to fetter judicial independence to an extent quite unparalleled elsewhere. Even on matters in which we are wont to leave a question to a judge's discretion, his use of it is subject to scrutiny by the pyramidal system of appeal to the Court of Appeal and the House of Lords who sit in panels of three and five and are therefore composed so as to counteract any individual idiosyncrasies in the lower tribunals or in one another.

There is, in fact, a widespread demand that the role of the judges should be extended. Most notable amongst these demands was the recent series of lectures by Lord Scarman, an articulate but wholly non-political figure if ever there was one. For reasons which I will be explaining I personally think he went too far, since, in administrative law, I believe he overestimated the extent to which decisions can be based on issues justiciable in the sense which I have explained. But the truth is that the intrusive decisions of the state as represented by minister, ministries and local and public authorities of different kinds have driven litigants on an increasing scale to seek from the courts decisions which must have sensitive political consequences. The courts cannot avoid this role, since, even if they decline jurisdiction or refuse to give the remedy sought, they are in fact taking a decision as controversial in its implications as if they allowed the remedy or assumed the jurisdiction.

In a large number of cases it is the Crown who comes to the courts invoking the law against the subject. The minority, I would fancy the rather small minority, of cases in which the courts decide in favour of the subject, is sufficiently large and covers a sufficiently wide range to attract considerable, and increasing, attention. These decisions are, in the nature of things, limited to disputes deriving from the actions of ministers or subordinate or local authorities, and not Acts of Parliament, which, whether construed narrowly or widely, cannot be rejected by the courts as illegal or *ultra vires*. But the distinction between Acts of Parliament and the acts of ministers or subordinate authority is becoming more and more artificial. To a great and greater degree, Parliament is becoming the House of Commons, the House of Commons is becoming the government majority and the government majority is a rubber stamp for government.

The fear often expressed by politicians, usually, though not always, on the left, that judges may be left to decide matters which their training does not suit them to discuss, is more and more unrealistic and, in my view, less and less in touch with public opinion. The real point is that the questions they decide should be in principle justiciable in the sense which I have tried to describe. It is immaterial that they involve consequences which are politically sensitive. The fear that the judges will be drawn into party politics is only well grounded when they are asked to intervene on matters which do not depend on ascertainable facts, or on legal rules which are not mainly objective in character. It is for this reason that I did not go along with part of Lord Scarman's view. It is not right that the courts should thrust far into the field of administrative law, for instance, the law of social security. But they should jealously pursue their undoubted right to invigilate the validity and fairness of administrative acts of ministers and local and subordinate authorities, and, in my view at least, there is no reason why, with great advantage to both parties, they should not be able to defend the rights of individuals and minorities where these deliberately or, more probably, by inadvertence are infringed by the Acts of the Central Legislative, or, if these come into being, subordinate or regional assemblies.

XVII

TWO CHEERS FOR CAPITALISM

One of the great paradoxes of our time is the continued prevalence of Marxism. All Marx's main theories have been disproved. The theory of surplus value is no longer held. The logic of the dialectic, based on Hegel, is pre-Darwinian. The prophecy that the rich will get richer and the poor poorer has proved laughably false. The belief that revolution would break out first in developed countries has been disproved by events. The doctrine that, after a short period of revolutionary dictatorship, followed by socialism, the state would fade away and a paradise follow, in which each would freely receive in accordance with his needs, and each gladly give in accordance with his abilities, has never been substantiated in any place where Marx's theories have been tried. In such countries the state has become stronger and stronger and, after more than two generations, shows not the slightest sign of fading or withering away. It is really astonishing that a man whose views have proved so completely, tragically, and often laughably wrong should still provide the economic and political orthodoxy of so much of the world, and be supposed by so many to provide a scientific basis for political thought.

Or is it? Quite clearly the appeal of Marxism in underdeveloped countries is at least as strong, and its views at least as plausible as when the Communist manifesto was first published in 1848. The paradox, if it be one, only really needs explaining in the free and capitalist West.

At first sight, of course, it is a paradox. I have already given my reasons for thinking that freedom is the real explanation of the vast improvement and expansion in every field of human activity since the Renaissance. Since capitalism is the natural consequence of intellectual and political freedom, and modern technology, which is itself the offspring of free enterprise and free scientific research, there must be at least two cheers for capitalism. But what is capitalism? Indeed, does it exist? And, if so, wherein lie its strength and its weakness? Of course to Marx, capitalism is the economic system dominated by Mr Gradgrind, or Dombey and Son, perhaps even by Marx's friend and co-author, Engels. But though these figures may still exist somewhere, like the coelacanth, in the depths of the distant economic oceans, they are very inconsiderable figures indeed. Even their modern analogues are usually genial rather than Scrooge-like figures, giving their friends a slice of the action without grinding down the face of their enemies. Even where it is personal and devious, the modern capitalism savours more of the gravy train than the song of the shirt.

But in truth of course, the colourful figures, even when, like the late Sir Denys Lowson, they become the objects of legitimate criticism, are exceptional to modern capitalism and not the rule. The typical modern capitalism is of a kind which would have appeared wholly incredible to Karl Marx. He had never met with it because in his day it did not exist, and he never envisaged it, because like everyone else, he could not foresee the future. The modern capitalism is the state capitalism of the Coal Board, British Rail or the Post Office, the private capitalism of ICI or Shell, or the mixed capitalism of British Leyland, Chrysler, BP or Rolls-Royce. It is worth pointing out that it is precisely in these vast concerns, in almost exact proportion as they are owned by the state, that Marxism still commands visible support amongst the workers, and where revolutionary activity is nearest the surface. This is another paradox, which is certainly not in accordance with Marxist doctrine, but may possibly offer some clue to the first.

When Marx wrote, the limited liability company was in its infancy. The doctrine of the Common Law was that if you engaged in trade, whether as an active, or as a sleeping partner, your liability was unlimited, and, because at that time the law was unkind to debtors, if the venture in which you had invested went broke you might find yourself with Mr Pickwick in the Fleet prison. As the prevailing philosophy favoured the investment of private savings as the main source of new capital, all over Europe laws were passed allowing the formation of limited liability companies, with shareholders and directors, policed by the courts, and soliciting subscriptions from the public in exchange for shares.

This, and not the industrial revolution, is the genesis of modern capitalism. At first no doubt it was very largely the old employers who made use of the new arrangements. But increasingly there grew up a new race of shareholders, nominally the joint owners of companies, but in reality treating their shares as property to be bought and sold on the Stock Exchange, and taking little part in management or policy. Once the initial investment is made, this kind of shareholder himself contributes nothing to the well-being of the company, except independence of the state and immunity from political control. If he does not approve of the policy of the directors, he usually sells his shares, and buys other shares in another company he thinks more likely to make a profit. He only rarely goes to company meetings. But he is far from being a parasite since his shares represent the legitimate reward for the original subscription, though probably it was not his, and, since he is less likely to be influenced by sentimental or political considerations than the government, his ownership of the shares represents an important bastion of freedom, and some guarantee of economic viability.

More and more, however, this second race of shareholder has given way to a third, the international investor, the bank, and above all the insurance company, and the pension scheme. Rather than an individual investor the modern shareholder is as likely to be a trade union, or a pension scheme, or an insurance company representing the collective interest of the holders of endowment policies or life insurance, or even the motorist's chance of securing an indemnity if he is sued in the courts after an accident, as an individual investor. He is far more likely to be one of these institutional property owners than either Tom Gradgrind or even James Goldsmith. This is modern private capitalism and anything less like the mythology of Karl Marx it is, at first sight, difficult to imagine. The third type of shareholder, unlike the second, begins again to take a healthy interest in policy and management, his holdings are too important for him not to do so.

On the other side of the picture are the Coal Board and the Post Office. Anomalously, the Post Office represents a long tradition of state trading for profit on the basis of monopoly. But the other boards, Railway, Road Transport, Gas, Electricity and the rest, represent the purchase compulsorily of the shareholdings of privately owned companies. The rights of the shareholder, whether he be private investor, institution, or close company proprietor are bought out. The essential structure of management and workers is retained, but with this solitary difference, that the new management, though nominally receiving a limited day-to-day autonomy, is in reality far more liable to political pressures, and therefore less able to guarantee economic efficiency than before the change of ownership. Originally, the workers thought that this would be to their advantage, which is why their trade unions have favoured nationalization. But the number of strikes, and the absence of profits in the nationalized industries are only too clear a proof that in no ascertained case has state capitalism created improved industrial relations or enhanced economic prospects, or better chances of secure employment or satisfactory wages for the workers. State capitalism, in the form in which it has developed in the West, is thus only a slightly less efficient version of private capitalism. In the East, it is far worse, since it is used by the state as a cynical means of keeping the workers in total subjection to the regime with the aid of secret police and military force.

We have still, however, not explained the original paradox. If this, acceptable or otherwise, is the face of modern capitalism, why does Marxism continue to be a credible philosophy, and why, sometimes in bizarre, heretical and deviant forms, does it sweep through the academic groves of the new universities and polytechnics like sparks through the stubble and excite the inflammable minds of the new, but sometimes immature, politicians of the Third World?

The reason, surely, is that, as it has developed either in state capitalism, private enterprise, or in a mixed form, the structure of modern capitalism sets up a conflict of interest or, in Marxist terms, a contradiction, between the interests of the workers in industry and the interest of the equity holder (in state capitalism the Exchequer) which management is quite unable to resolve. In theory, at least, in state capitalism, management must consider both the public interest and that of the workers. But it is given no guidance as to what happens when they do not coincide, which they seldom do. In mixed and private capitalism, as the law stands at the moment, the management have in theory a straight remit to pursue the interests of the equity owners, that is, the shareholders. It makes very little difference in the end, because enlightened self-interest makes it impossible for management or equity holders to disregard the interests of the workers, though perfectly easy to disregard the interests of the public, except in so far as they are protected by consumer resistance to the product, or legislative interference from Parliament.

But there is this difference between the new capitalism and the old. Gradgrind, Dombey, or Scrooge might be unattractive characters. But you could at least talk to them. The mill owner would know his workers, and so did Lord Nuffield whilst he still worked in Longwall Street. But these vast concerns are different. As often as not the shareholder is another limited company. The ultimate holders of the equity, the holding company's shareholders, are quite anonymous, and their interests so vast, and their workers so numerous, that their decisions might well come from the top of Mount Olympus, and have been devised by Zeus, the Gatherer of Clouds, and his consort, Hera. The face of modern capitalism may be acceptable but it is not visible, and this is so whether the equity is owned by the state, an anonymous group of private shareholders, a trade union or the Prudential. Nor can the worker say: 'Come back Tom Gradgrind, all is forgiven.' Tom Gradgrind no longer exists, or if he does, he is living on his compensation in the Isle of Man, and anyhow never has enough capital to interest himself in the vast colossi of modern industry.

The Marxist 'contradiction' which still bedevils the new capitalism may be quite different from the old. But it is still a contradiction, and it is enhanced rather than minimized by the structure of modern trade unionism, which has, on the whole, altered less than modern capitalism. The old mill owner or the old mine owner was not only approachable by his workers. If only to some degree, he, and they, had also the common interest in the success of the mill or pit.

Without it, neither could earn a living. But the modern trade union official has no necessary interest in the success of a particular concern. His organization is based on the District, or the National Headquarters, not on the plant, and in the plant he may very well represent only a minority of the workers with interests showing a distinct Marxist contradiction with some of the others. The idea that there should be loyalty to the plant sometimes arises when there is a threat of closure from on high. But the structure does not encourage it whether in the breasts of management, workers, or trade union officials whilst it remains a going concern.

It may well be that the future of modern capitalism lies in restoring loyalty to the plant, human faces to management, plant loyalty to workers' representatives. The process may involve original thinking and somewhat traumatic experiences in carrying it into effect. But we can hardly go on as we are if we wish to compete with Japan, whose wily little inhabitants have already seen the point.

XVIII

TWO CHEERS FOR WELFARE

No one gets very far in a political discussion without some discussion of the welfare state. I have already rejected utilitarianism, which, in its developed form, proposes the general welfare as the sole criterion by which legislation must be judged as unfair to individuals and minorities. But it would be an odd sort of state which regarded the general welfare as irrelevant to policy. I must point out, however, that the expression welfare in this context does not mean the same thing as 'welfare' in the expression 'welfare state'. The general welfare is something vague and diffused. The welfare state offers concrete benefits to some individuals, at the expense of others who, directly or indirectly, pay for them. This may or may not match the utilitarian criterion, and although the critics do not often find their way into print in this country, they are vocal elsewhere, and I have often heard the welfare state blamed for the sad decline in our national fortunes. Benefits of this sort, it is argued, sap self-reliance, discourage thrift and enterprise, induce fecklessness, encourage scrounging and downright dishonesty, attract undesirable immigrants, and these arguments are sometimes corroborated by unhappy examples of blundering bureaucracy or individual abuse.

I must make it clear at once that I have no use for this opinion, despite some superficial plausibility and a certain measure of popular appeal. In the form in which we know it, the welfare state was not born in the hour of Mr Attlee's election victory in 1945, nor on the day of publication of the Beveridge Report in 1942, nor even on the passing of the budget of 1909. The care of the sick, the education of the young, the relief of poverty and old age both by private charity and public provision have from time immemorial been part of the philosophy of this island. The question is not whether, but how, at what level of excellence, and at the expense of what other desirable goals. It is a natural corollary of the abundance created by the freedom of a capitalist society that the spread should be wider and the level higher than ever before. It is those who are in work, and adult and in health who must bear the burden of their own and others' insurance. There is nothing else and no one else who can be made to bear it. The product of industry bears all. There is no basin of gold somewhere above the cloud cover consisting of the investments of a parasitic rentier class which can carry the burden. It is the product of industry which must do so, and the channel through which it flows is, in one form or another, the channel of taxation, the channel of personal saving or the channel of private charity. The question is in what form and at what level the product of industry is to be tapped.

I do not accept that relative security is something which in itself saps enterprise. This is equivalent to saying that what encourages enterprise is the fear of poverty. This does not accord with my own experience of life or with my reading of history. No doubt you sap enterprise by denying it any hope of legitimate reward. This is one of the most powerful arguments against the popular socialism of the day. But it is quite another thing to argue that fear of poverty encourages enterprise, or that to remove that fear saps it. The contrary is often true. It is precisely the poverty stricken, the handicapped, the slum dweller, who being without hope, and without help, and often without skills, become feckless and listless, give up trying, or seek improvidently to improve their fortunes by gambling or crime or to drown their sorrows in drink. Whatever else is true about the welfare state, I do not believe that anyone who has visited countries where it does not exist, or reads the history of Victorian society before it existed in a developed form here, can fail to form the view that a welfare state is beneficial both to those who receive the benefits, and to those who provide them, that it gives security and hope to those in need, assists them to plan their future, to live thrifty and rewarding lives, and to engage in activities with a view to improving their fortunes. I write this as one who is often sickened by talk of a compassionate and caring society uttered by those who are really only concerned to advance their own popularity by spending other people's money. But I am quite sure that the welfare state, whatever may be said against it, is not a cause of fecklessness and demoralization. High taxation with low reward is such a cause. The relief of hardship is not.

I also point to the economic stability which it tends to engender. If every time a man falls ill or out of work he has to stop spending altogether the fluctuations in demand are accentuated. Enlightened self-interest on the part of the majority demands that these fluctuations should be reduced and a fair level of expenditure maintained.

I am not very fond of the expression 'social justice' which is commonly used by those whose interest it is to foster envy, hatred and malice, and all uncharitableness between the classes. But, when all is said and done, there are moral considerations which cannot be ignored, particularly in a state of full employment.

The physically handicapped, whether by accident, disease, or congenital weakness, the old and the young are, in the nature of things unable to benefit by the qualities demanded for success in a highly competitive world. It has been accepted for a long time, indeed, on an unorganized basis since the Middle Ages, that these are matters which must be catered for in a well-organized society, and the idea that they can be left either entirely or mainly to the haphazard efforts of thrift, private benevolence or charitable trusts is not really sensible. But it must be said very plainly that there is nothing sacrosanct about our present arrangements. I can myself see no alternative to the finance of education out of taxation if provision is to be at all adequate and evenly spread. But our methods of financing the health and social security systems, and housing, leave much to be desired, and in fact compare very unfavourably with some continental schemes which give higher benefits and are far more rationally contrived. Our present plans derive almost directly from the recommendations of the Beveridge Committee and were founded on the supposition of a post-war level of unemployment of 10% (on the pre-war method of computation) or 8% (on the post-war method). There seems no good reason why a fully employed worker or his employer should not bear the same proportion of these charges as elsewhere in Europe, or should not be able at least in part to contract out and contribute to a special scheme more precisely tailored to his needs.

Throughout my life our domestic housing has been a long history of under-provision and shortage, and the pillars of government policy throughout have been rent restriction, security of tenure, and municipally financed and subsidized accommodation for rent. It is a system which has no theoretical advantages in peace time, except in so far as the weekly tenancy and eviction without court order are no longer socially acceptable. So far as its practical operation is considered, it can only be said not to have shown, after an adequate trial, to produce a reasonable stock of accommodation at appropriate prices. It is now possible to make comparison with many other democratic societies in Europe and elsewhere. It is now demonstrable that better provision for the social services and benefits can be made by relating the use of facilities and the cost of them more directly to individual needs.

A fully employed society ought, in theory at least, to be organized in such a way that the worker or his employer should provide direct insurance against sickness, unemployment, accident and old age, and should pay the full cost of housing. Taxation, which is a relatively crude and expensive way of channelling the product of industry into desirable ends, would be left to pay for the education of children and for the handicapped and other classes who have fallen by the wayside. If the insurance schemes were genuinely funded instead of being used simply as a form of taxation they might very well prove a valuable source of public and private investment. No one would wish to go back to the very inadequate health provision prior to the National Health Service, but I always thought that the destruction of the approved societies which were part of the old apparatus was an expensive mistake, and that the present centrally controlled organization both of the hospitals and of the service generally is relatively costly, inefficient, and unnecessarily uniform for a population whose needs vary, and for whom different types of provision and a more personal service would have been preferable. Our present organization, with which, I fear, we are saddled for a very long time to come, is yet another example of the evils of overcentralization and the cult of uniformity inspired by an anxiety to avoid the recurrence of social conditions which no longer exist or can exist.

One other point on the welfare state remains to be made. From the publication of the Beveridge Report onwards, conservative opinion in Britain, and even more in the United States, has tended to attack and criticize the conception of publicly organized social services as socialist in nature.

I do not wish to engage now in a purely semantic discussion on the meaning of socialism which obviously means very different things to different people. I only wish to make two points to those who, like me, favour the private organization of industry, a plural society, multiplicity of parties, and evolutionary politics.

The first is that from the point of view of conservatism with a small 'c', the effect of this attitude has been to give the devil some of the best tunes. My experience as a politician has been that among the reputable arguments which turn voters to vote for socialist rather than free enterprise candidates is this ungenerous attitude towards publicly organized or supported social services provided at a level which satisfies contemporary tastes and standards of comfort and security. Indeed, a great number of people who have not reflected at all deeply about the nature of the subject would actually admit that they have joined the Labour Party simply because they believe in the necessity for services on this scale, and associate the Labour Party exclusively with the desire to provide them.

But this is not so, and this is the second point I wish to make. So far from being the enemies of one another, I believe that publicly organized social services on an adequate scale, and privately owned industry should be complementary and that the failure to realize this is one of the underlying causes of our present economic troubles. Those who have voted for the Labour Party have thought they were voting for adequate social services only to find that they were voting for a party with a militantly Marxist wing dedicated to the nationalization of one industry after another. In attacking the present level of expenditure, and the gross inequalities and injustices of personal taxation, Conservative speakers and writers have allowed themselves to be drawn into general criticisms and arguments calculated to give rise to reasonable doubts about the sincerity of their adhesion to generous social provision, however financed. The result is that their general and proper espousal of the cause of free enterprise in the name of liberty has tended to be obscured. This is an ideological mistake which has been repeated by the Republican Party in the United States, but not, on the whole, by the Christian Democratic parties on the continent of Europe. If Conservatives wish to remain a national party they must learn to avoid this error for the future.

XIX

ONE CHEER FOR
INCOMES POLICY

Many years ago, in the House of Commons, I remember
pressing Sir Stafford Cripps, who was then in charge of
economic policy, on the necessity for incomes policy. I was
much younger then, and I am not quite sure what I meant.
What I think I meant was that the government of the day
ought to have some idea what the level of income ought to
be, after tax, for different types of work. I am sure that I
did not mean any form of statutory control. Cripps's answer
was pretty resolute. He said it could not be done without
direction of labour, which, save for a short aberration during
the Attlee Government, has never been seriously contemplated in time of peace.

But ever since then, in one sense or another incomes
policy has constantly cropped up as a necessity, has been
fairly regularly attempted, and has almost as regularly
failed, and its proponents thereafter cast out into the electoral
wilderness.

The theoretical arguments against it are overwhelming.
Right-wing and left-wing critics have vied with one another
to condemn it. Free bargains, as freely arrived at, are as
much part of the established ideology of the unions as they
are of Mr Enoch Powell. Successive parties have achieved
office on the express undertaking to avoid it, an undertaking
which has as regularly been broken. The pressure for a
wages policy has usually come from the Civil Service and our
creditors. The pressure against it has come from the grass
roots. It has been adopted by government under the compulsion of economic crisis, and as regularly abandoned by
parties when they pass from power to opposition. There
have been declarations of intent, guiding lights, wise men,
Boards concerned with prices and incomes, phases one, two
and three, plateaux, freezes, and latterly social contracts and

guide lines. There have been differences of phraseology and detail. All have had fundamental points of resemblance. They have, where possible, fought shy of calling the spade a spade. They have adopted the pretence of voluntarism, and the reality of compulsion. They have been adopted with the intention of being temporary, and they have proved even more temporary than they were intended to be.

The reason for failure has been twofold, the constant pressure of prices and the necessity for differential rewards corresponding to differences in enterprise, diligence and skill and to the changing demand for particular types of labour. But the vicious circle has never ceased to revolve. Wage demands have led to inflation. Inflation has led to a demand either for a price freeze, or a wage freeze or both. The demand has been met. The result has proved intolerable and unsustainable. The freeze has melted. The accumulated dissatisfaction has resulted in an ugly rush to raise prices and wages. The inflation has begun again, and the cycle is complete.

For my own part, I believe that the underlying cause is the insatiable human illusion that it is possible to eat your cake and have it. People will not believe that you cannot freeze prices in time of peace without creating bankruptcies, shortage, unemployment and a black market. They will not believe that unless it is coupled with improved efficiency you cannot raise wages in one sector without creating unemployment or inadequate expansion in another, and that inadequate expansion allied with increased demand lead inevitably to an excess of imports and currency depreciation. For a time, it has been possible to control imports physically as Mr Butler did in the early 1950s. This, of course, is an agreeable expedient, since it results in the export of the resultant unemployment, and the cushioning of home industry against foreign competition always regarded as unfair in proportion as it is successful. It is difficult to persuade those who benefit from import controls that their policy is unpopular abroad, and, since in the nature of things they are not themselves exporters, they tend to underestimate the danger of retaliation.

None of the pressure groups demanding wage or price freezes, physical controls, or other forms of government intervention are prepared to accept that their remedies are self-defeating and that they are perpetuating the vicious circle which has led to their own demands. It may be that Adam Smith was right. But it may also be that his economic policies are impossible in a democracy which no more wishes to be educated in economic laws than it wishes to learn the differential calculus. If so, of course, in the end democracy will collapse.

At least a subsidiary cause of the vicious circle is the constant oscillation between government and opposition to which the two-party system has given rise, operating on the power of government to increase monetary supply. If the government did not have so wide a power to increase the money supply, or if the polarity created by the two-party system did not operate so as to drive governments so persistently to adopt the line of least popular resistance, it might well be that the vicious circle would operate less viciously. It did operate differently before the war. That was the importance of the return of the gold standard, so severely condemned today as the cause of the terrible unemployment of the thirties. Whatever its defects the gold standard prevented the constant resort to devaluation which characterized the continental currencies before Dr Schacht. No doubt also there are some who believe that a similar effect could be achieved notwithstanding the floating pound, and I suppose that, if applied rigorously enough, unemployment and high import prices could be used to achieve this result. But the nerve of successive governments has always cracked before the moment has come. The nearest it came to holding since the war was during Mr Jenkins's Chancellorship when, at the price of a million unemployed, an enormous surplus was built up. Its dissipation during the early years of the Heath Government was a constant source of derision at the time. But I notice that the Jenkins policy was an experiment not repeated under Mr Healey.

A government backed only by the members of a single party seems to achieve financial rectitude only when foreign creditors and Treasury officials begin to call the tune. By that time the pound has fallen several points further in relation to stronger currencies. After such a fall no one has ever known it rise to its previous levels. The most that has ever been achieved so far is a temporary halt at a lower level, as the vicious circle moves from one dead centre to another. The relatively gloomy conclusion is that the vicious circle is due less to economic causes than the operation of our present democratic structure.

In short, our weakness is psychological, political, and constitutional, and not economic. In part it is due to the uninhibited use of monopoly power by large unions, in part by the public's inability to recognize that it is impossible to freeze prices without causing shortage and unemployment and restricting growth, and impossible to increase incomes without lowering the standard of life of others unless the increase is matched by an increase of production.

But the effect is rendered inevitable by the party battle in the House of Commons in which each successive opposition party undermines the ability of the government to pursue restrictive economic policies to the point at which they begin to yield results.

XX

ELECTIVE DICTATORSHIP

So far we are left with a paradox. Since the sixteenth century and except in time of war, never has a government possessed more power than it has today. Never has it spent more money, employed a greater army of people, imposed so many regulations, passed so many laws, raised so much in taxation, operated in so many spheres, or exercised a wider patronage.

Yet, at the same time, never does it seem, at least for many years, to have commanded so little respect, achieved so few successes, exacted so little loyalty, and perhaps imposed so low a standard of obedience.

Before the eclipse of Britain, how proud we were of everything British. Now there is scarcely an institution or attitude which does not come in for criticism, scarcely a policy in which there is not a demand for reform. The time has come to examine the structures which have given rise to this paradox.

The constitutional law of this island is based on the ancient prerogatives of the Crown, and the various Acts of Parliament by which these have been modified or extended. We have always possessed a strong central government, and when the powers of Crown and Parliament are united under a strong administration, the legal powers of government are virtually unlimited. The limitations are moral and political, and are the result of conscious restraint or public opinion. They are not limitations imposed by law. In theory Parliament is supreme. There is nothing legally it cannot do, and practically nothing which, at one time or another, it has not done. It has prolonged its own life. It has taken away the lives or liberties of its fellow citizens without the semblance of a fair trial. It has confiscated property. It has ratified revolutions.

In this we are almost unique. The Congress of the United States, the French Assembly, the Bonn Legislature, the

Diet of Japan, the federal legislature of Switzerland, do not possess these powers or anything like them. Nor do the Parliaments of the various members of the Commonwealth to whom we have given independence. All possess powers limited by a constitution, which they have not the right to exceed. Only we live under the authority of a rule absolute in theory if tolerable in practice.

Its powers are restrained only by the consciences of its members, the checks and balances of its different parts and the need, recognized in practice if capable in theory of being deferred, for periodical elections. In our lifetime the use of its powers has continuously increased, and the checks and balances have been rendered increasingly ineffective by the concentration of their effective operation more and more in the House of Commons, in the government side of the House of Commons, in the Cabinet within the government side, and to some extent in the Prime Minister within the Cabinet. The sovereignty of Parliament, absolute in theory, has become more and more the sovereignty of the House of Commons, and like all absolute rulers, the House of Commons, having more and more to do, and in consequence less and less time within which to do it, is becoming more and more the tool of its professional advisers, more and more intolerant of criticism, and less and less in control of the detail of what is done in its name. Because the House of Commons and its shortcomings are so much at the centre of our present embarrassments it is worth spending a little time examining the title deeds by which it governs.

The House of Commons reached its present position because it came to be regarded as the guardian of our liberties. These it vindicated successfully against the Barons, against the medieval Church, against the Crown, against the Whig aristocrats of the eighteenth and against the manufacturing plutocracy of the nineteenth centuries. Until recently no one regarded the House of Commons as itself a source of potential danger. So powers were willingly confided in it, and no safeguards other than the obligation to hold elections exacted in exchange. It does not follow that today the unlimited powers which were once thought safely entrusted to a guardian of liberty are now as wisely allowed to remain in the hands of what has become an instrument of government.

Since publishing my Dimbleby lecture, I have been taken to task for describing our system of government as an elective dictatorship. Indeed, one critic, possibly more enthusiastic than wise, ventured to describe the expression as a contradiction in terms. I remain wholly unrepentant. A very large collection of dictators from Pisistratus to Hitler have begun by being elected, or like Henry VIII, have used Parliaments or referenda to justify tyrannical rule. The forms of democracy may long continue (as they did under the Roman principate) long after the reality has disappeared. I have never suggested that freedom is dead in Britain. But it has diminished, and a principal cause of its impairment has been, in truth, the absolute legislative power confided in Parliament, concentrated in the hands of a government armed with a Parliamentary majority, briefed and served by the professionalism of the Civil Service, and given a more than equal chance of self-perpetuation by the adroit use of the power of dissolution. When such a government is indoctrinated with the false political doctrine of mandate and manifesto, or when it is perpetuated in office until a suitable moment for dissolution occurs by an unprincipled bargain by another party equally threatened with electoral defeat, the expression 'elective dictatorship' is certainly not a contradiction in terms, though it may contain an element of warning of where we are tending rather than statement of despair at where we have arrived.

The House of Commons is dominated by parties, traditionally two or not much more, but now, about nine in number. Broadly speaking, the same is true of constituencies. The party organizations in the House determine in practice the result of almost every division. In constituencies the vote of the electors for or against particular candidates is determined by the colour of their badge, and only to a very limited extent by their achievements, their qualities or their personal character.

As Disraeli long ago observed, it is no good complaining of this as if it were an abuse. It is inherent in the system of Parliamentary government. It is the only way in which coherence and consistency can be given to politics. Collective decisions of policy and political principles attributable to parties are the only means by which the electorate can exercise control over what goes on in the House of Commons or a significant choice on broad public issues.

But, while it is no good complaining of the fact, it becomes necessary to discover how candidates are chosen by their parties, in what manner members are elected by the voters, and how their powers are exercised once they are at work. The results of such an enquiry are not altogether reassuring. The selection of candidates is, of necessity, in the hands of a caucus. We have no system of primaries, and I personally do not desire to introduce them. But the caucus, necessarily consisting of a tiny minority of the electorate, has a disproportionate amount of power, particularly in a so-called 'safe' seat, where, in selecting a candidate, they virtually select a member. Before the Maxwell Fyfe reforms, selection in the Conservative Party went all too often to the highest bidder, the test being the amount of the subscription he was prepared to give to the constituency. When I was first interviewed by the Chairman of the Party in about 1936 with a view to becoming a candidate, I was told that, although personally acceptable, I had no prospect of selection unless I offered £400 a year. In one East Anglian constituency the figure subscribed was said to be £3000. At about the same time the late Mr Cunningham Reid bought the Marylebone seat almost literally like a pound of tea. These bad days have gone with the war and Conservative candidates are now democratically approved by the constituency organization, having first passed through ordeals by Central Office, local selection committee, and party executive. But all these committees are subject to fancies, vulnerable to cliques and feuds and, like all party activists, occasionally favour extremes of one sort or another.

In the Labour Party some seats are held like feudal baronies by particular trade unions, who subsequently sponsor and subsidize the member so that he is scarcely free to exercise an independent vote. Some constituencies, particularly the safe ones, seem to be peculiarly vulnerable to infiltration by extremist groups, on occasion not even loyal to the party itself, who may even claim a right to control the exercise of the member's conscience as he votes in the House, and sometimes even when he supports the party leadership. None of this is satisfactory.

The electorate is itself markedly moderate in its views. But where the caucus is infiltrated, a few extremists have it in their power to deny them the right to vote for a moderate candidate.

The method of voting at an election is, of course, first past the post. The case for and against proportional representation is well known and I do not wish to argue it here, particularly as I am more than a trifle agnostic on the subject. But the result of the present method is indisputable. It is now normal for governments to represent a minority of electors, and even a minority of those who actually voted. I have myself no particular objection to this, but on two conditions. In the absence of a coherent majority for any one party, it seems to me to be rational for the executive government of a country to reflect the views of the largest organized minority. It also seems to me to be highly desirable for Members of Parliament to represent single member constituencies.

But, whilst I can see the advantage of an executive government being formed in this way and supported by an elective majority of members in a House constituted in this way, I can see no advantage whatever in that government, and that House, being given unlimited powers of legislation. There must be a point at which it is prudent to return to the theory of the separation of powers, adopted by the American fathers in conscious imitation of what they believed to be the original British practice. That point must be reached when a government elected by a small minority of votes, and with a slight majority in the House, regards itself as entitled, and, according to its more extreme supporters, bound to carry out every proposal in its election manifesto. This has happened more than once in the past few years, and it seems to me that at almost any cost we must ensure that it cannot happen again.

As will be seen, my preferred solution would be to have a second chamber proportionately elected side-by-side with the House of Commons, not entitled to settle the political colour of the executive government or to control finance, but entitled to have the other functions of the existing House of Lords, and more than its existing powers. Whether this be acceptable or not, we should surely need our heads examined if we were to go on with the system by which members, selected as candidates by existing methods of nomination, and elected as members by existing methods of voting, are entitled to vote general legislation without adequate control, legal or political, on the use of their powers.

But I have not quite done with the House of Commons yet. In my Dimbleby lecture I pointed out the extent to which the sheer volume of work makes it quite impossible for a modern House of Commons to carry out its task in a conscientious manner. When Gladstone was Prime Minister, he was able to spend five months of the year at Hawarden in North Wales. I suppose the House of Commons of his day was actually in recess for seven months in the year. As late as 1911, the great reforming Liberal administration of Asquith was content with a mere 450 pages of legislation placed upon the statute book. Under Sir Harold Wilson one comparable year yielded about 3000 pages of statute, and another 10,000 pages of statutory instrument. Who can pretend that a volume of legislation of this kind can be adequately scrutinized? And, if it were, what sort of representatives do we expect to elect if they were to devote sufficient time to this immense flow?

In my view, the professional politician should be the exception rather than the rule amongst MPs, if only because a professional politician cannot be representative of a constituency, which however constituted, is not composed of professional politicians. There are other reasons equally compelling. A professional politician is thrown on the street if he is turned out. If married and with a family he cannot afford to affront the party whips or offend his local constituency association or perhaps the local branch of the NUM or the Transport Union. He ceases to be the responsible representative of a free constituency, and, if he is not careful, he soon develops into a disreputable party hack. There are too many such hacks in the present-day House of Commons.

Then again the parts of the United Kingdom are unequally represented. Ulster members represent about 100,000 voters, but only count in a division as much as Scottish members who represent only about 50,000, or English members who represent about 60,000. But these figures again represent extremely unequal distributions. Some of the safe seats in the Labour-held cities in England hold about 20,000 voters. Some of the Conservative or marginal seats on the periphery represent 100,000 or more. Although the Boundary Commissions have stopped the worst kind of gerrymandering, any ultimate redistribution depends in the last resort on a vote in the House of Commons. Twice, at least in my Parliamentary career, I have had personally to complain about direct gerrymandering by Labour Home Secretaries, and the Crossman diaries show that I was not far wrong in these matters. Moreover the over-representation of Scotland is to some extent guaranteed by the Act of Union.

The pressure on Parliamentary time leads, from time to time, to demands for a reform of the procedure of the House, or for extended sittings in the mornings as well as the afternoons, or for the transaction of even more business by standing committees, who can number fewer than twenty members. But the effect of this would simply be to rivet the chains of elective dictatorship more firmly upon us all. We do not need to assist government business, but to reduce its volume, and this can be done in a whole series of different ways, but not by extending the hours of sitting or diminishing discussion on the floor of the House. Parliament must learn to do less work. We do not need more government but less. The remedy for an excessive burden of work is not to hurry through more work more quickly, but actually to do less business. This could be achieved in three ways. The first is reducing the total quantity of legislation and seeing that it is more fully discussed. The second is by devolving on lower tiers of government work which is now done of necessity in Westminster. The third would be to reduce the actual numbers of Members of Parliament to correspond with the lower volume of work. This would reduce the number of speeches, and the amount of time wasted in repetitive debate.

But the real necessity is to limit the unlimited powers of the legislature, partly by establishing a new system of checks and balances, partly by devolution, and partly by restricting the power of Parliament to infringe the rights of minorities and individuals. In other words we need a new constitution, and like all new constitutions its terms must be reduced to writing and defined by law.

XXI

CONSTITUTIONS, WRITTEN AND UNWRITTEN

We are so accustomed to praising the merits of our constitution that we tend to forget what these merits are and why they are so praiseworthy. But, when we are asked to give our reasons, one of the first expressions which rises so spontaneously to our lips is the adjective 'unwritten'.

What do we mean by this? I suggest we mean several things of very unequal value. But if we mean that our constitution has never been reduced to writing this can be very misleading. We still find Magna Carta (as revised in 1297) amongst our statutes. So also do we find the Petition of Right, the Bill of Rights, the Act of Settlement, the Act of Union with Scotland, the Catholic Emancipation Act and the Statute of Westminster. These are only a few. So far as the unwritten part of the constitution is concerned, only the extent of the Queen's prerogative and the powers of Parliament are completely or almost completely unwritten, and the latter are as clear as if they are written, since it has been long established that the powers of Parliament are wholly unlimited by any legal fetters except those which the two Houses have chosen to impose upon themselves.

What then do we mean when we claim as a feature of our constitution that it is unwritten? I will suggest that we mean several things, and the first is that it is of immemorial antiquity and that it has grown and not been contrived as a coherent whole.

This is true of a number of institutions, the Papacy for example, or the Church of England. The Methodist Church and the fifth French Republic or the Federal Republic of Germany are examples of another kind of institution, the contrived. Of course, human institutions do not neatly fit into either category. The constitution of the United States of America, for instance, although a clear example of the 'contrived' or 'written' type, has many features, after two hundred years of working, of the 'unwritten' type. For instance, it is as much a convention of the constitution of the United States that the President's Cabinet should not at the same time be members of Congress as that the members of the British Cabinet should all be Members of Parliament in one House or the other.

There are advantages in both types. But there is no doubt that the glamour and mystique attaching to a traditional constitution is an immense asset in times of stress, a source of great stability and confidence, a guarantee of continuity in the midst of change, the hallmark of legitimacy, a unifying influence. However many the changes we may wish to make, I would not have these assets dissipated, or lose the immense power and strength of tradition. For seven hundred years first England, then Britain and finally the United Kingdom, have been governed by the Crown in Parliament. I would not have it otherwise.

There is another sense in which we praise the unwritten character of our laws and constitution. It is a feature of written constitutions or codes that their terms should be exact and their terms precise. An unwritten constitution or legal system is like a growing plant. It has its growing points and its withering points. It is, as it were, furry at the edges. On the boundaries of what is permissible or impermissible you do not know quite where you stand, though you do know that you overstep the boundaries at your peril. There is room for advance, and for retreat, and for a temporary stance in uncertainty. No one, for instance, can have known when Queen Anne used for the last time the Norman French formula '*La royne s'avisera*' refusing her royal assent to a Bill that this would be the last time that this was ever done, and that it could never be done again without a breach of the constitution. When King George I, knowing little English, and conversing with his Prime Minister, Robert Walpole, who knew no German, in somewhat inaccurate Latin, ceased to preside at his Cabinet Councils, he did not know, any more than did Walpole, that he was setting the pattern of a new type of Cabinet government which would spread from Britain throughout the world. The participation by the reigning monarch in politics withered away slowly, and, as we saw in the Queen's address at the beginning of the Jubilee celebrations, has even now a slightly ambiguous meaning. The political impartiality of Mr Speaker and the judges was established but slowly through the eighteenth century to the present day. There is great merit in advance by trial and error, and I myself would never wish to reduce the influence of judge made and customary law in matters where its limitations and characteristics can be seen to operate to the public benefit.

But there is a third sense in which we praise the unwritten nature of our constitution which, I believe, is far more open to question. Most countries with 'written' constitutions recognize a distinction between constitutional or basic law as defined by the 'written' document and ordinary law or legislation. These nations make changes in the constitutional legal rules more difficult to achieve than modifications of ordinary law, usually by restricting the extent to which they can be brought about by a simple Act of the legislature, and by prescribing a special procedure for constitutional change which includes a method designed to consult the will of the people and requiring a more decisive majority than a plain 51% to secure approval. It is no coincidence that one of the earlier acts of the Federal legislature of Western Germany with the memory of Hitler still fresh was to establish a basic law or *grundgesetz* of such a kind. These constitutions were described by the first Lord Birkenhead, sitting as Lord Chancellor in a Canadian appeal, as 'controlled' rather than 'written' constitutions. He contrasted these 'controlled' constitutions with our own unwritten constitution which he described as 'uncontrolled'.

By this he meant that over the centuries it has come to be established in Britain that there is no limit whatever to the legislative powers of Parliament. Only the other day it was decided that even a private Act of Parliament could not be questioned in the courts, even when the aggrieved party complained that it had been obtained by fraud, or passed solely owing to a mistake of fact in one or both of the two Houses. In this respect Britain is unique amongst developed nations, except, I believe, New Zealand, and, possibly, Israel. There is no right, however sacred, of the individual or of a minority which cannot be infringed or abolished by an Act of Parliament. The sole sanctions restricting this almost unique authority rest in the consciences of the members of each House, the influence of public opinion, the necessity for periodical general elections (although Parliament can even prolong its own life and has in fact done so within my own lifetime), and the power of Parliament to reverse or amend its own legislation.

There is no doubt that this legislative omnipotence, usually dressed up in the complimentary phrase 'the sovereignty of Parliament', has been extremely useful in the past and has afforded an extremely valuable element of flexibility in time of need. It saved us from the necessity of a general election in 1940 and subsequent war years. It enabled Parliament during the war to authorize the most dictatorial acts by the executive, including imprisonment without trial, military conscription, the requisition of property without recourse to the ordinary courts, the restriction of jury trials, and all the apparatus of wartime regulation and control. No one can be sure that, in the turbulent modern world of which we are part, these powers may not be needed again. I therefore approach my criticism of them with a certain degree of caution, and even diffidence.

However, one must remember that, with the exceptions which I have mentioned, neither of which is typical, no other free country has found it necessary to confer these powers or shown any signs of wishing to do so, and when we have conferred freedom on our former colonies and dominions we have not in the main found it possible to export this peculiar feature of the Westminster model. It must be conceded therefore, that, unless we credit the British Member of Parliament with a comparative absence of original sin, the burden of proof rests on those who wish to justify this particular feature of the 'sovereignty of Parliament' rather than on those who would prefer to dispense with it.

I suppose that, if the matter rested there, I might well be amongst those who preferred the status quo, and, for the greater part of my life, I certainly numbered myself in their company. As I have said our 'unwritten' constitution has served us well. Written constitutions have many defects. In an era of change, their comparative rigidity is often irksome.

Their restrictions sometimes lead to a welter of litigation. I believe that in India before Mrs Gandhi's state of emergency, there were about 250,000 challenges to the validity of actions by the executive and legislature every year. So, if matters had not changed for us, I would consider myself as much a conservative about this matter as I am in most other things.

But matters have changed for us. In the first place there is the immense extent to which the state has widened its activities in recent years. This is only partly measured by the huge bulk of its legislative activity. Even the bulk itself means that much legislation goes through which, from sheer inadvertence, brings much injustice and anomaly in its train. But the state now intrudes into almost every activity of private life. The state produces, sells, manufactures, it transports, delivers, employs, distributes, regulates, educates, cares for the sick, nannies the healthy, governesses the careless, buries the dead, provides for the old, limits wealth, pursues us all from the cradle to the grave. I am not saying that all of this is bad. Much is undoubtedly good. Much more is quite inevitable. Only a relatively small proportion is certainly bad. But powers which were tolerable when exercised on the much more modest scale of the 1900s may require much more careful scrutiny and restriction in the quite different conditions of the 1970s. Differences in scale become quite distinctly differences in kind when they proceed beyond a point.

This, however, is only the beginning of the case for a new constitution, 'written' in the sense that Lord Birkenhead meant when he described such constitutions as 'controlled'. In the first place Britain has now adhered to a number of European and other international conventions, of which the most important from this point of view are the European Convention on Human Rights and the EEC. The British Courts are already bound by statute to apply Community law to the decision of some cases in preference to Common Law or even statute, and thus, in this limited sphere, are vested with the very power to strike down Acts of Parliament which the opponents of change so much fear.

But this power is likely, in the circumstances of the European Convention, and similar treaties which are enforceable, to prove a benefit since our own courts are quicker, cheaper and more accessible. The European Convention is enforceable by the European Court, but not, as matters stand, in the British Courts. The result has been that, although probably among the more liberal regimes even in Europe, by far the most numerous complaints in the European Court have in fact been directed against our country.

This has been both expensive and humiliating. Moreover the delays and expense undoubtedly operate to deprive litigants of the rights which they would probably exercise if they were available for assertion in our domestic courts. Indeed, one of the arguments strangely advanced by the present Lord Chancellor against Lord Wade's Bill to embody the Convention in domestic law was precisely that its passage into law would produce a flood of litigation. When I challenged him on this on the ground that it was strange in a Labour Lord Chancellor to use the power of the purse to deter potential complaints, he replied that he only referred to frivolous complaints. Unfortunately the power of the purse, like the rain, restricts the just equally with the unjust, and more particularly the just, because, being rational, they are the more likely to be deterred. To modern government much complaint seems frivolous where effect cannot be given to it in the courts.

But it is not only in the field of human rights that these arguments apply. Rightly or wrongly, I am convinced that, if we wish to retain the unity of the United Kingdom, we shall be driven to set up subordinate legislative assemblies in Northern Ireland, Scotland, probably in Wales, and, I would expect, in various parts of England. Hitherto devolution or 'home rule' bills have foundered on two rocks. The first has been the set of anomalies created by the institution of assemblies with limited rights to legislate over particular geographical areas of a state which remains unitary elsewhere. The second has been the temptation to conflict inherent in the conception of a subordinate assembly with a limited power to legislate over defined fields of policy and a central assembly with an unlimited power to legislate in all matters including the devolved subjects. The danger of political conflict in these circumstances is, I believe, obvious. But the legislative confusion is also likely to be considerable.

138

Even in a fully federalized system as it exists, for instance, in Canada and Australia, when provincial and central legislatures operate theoretically in separate fields, the legislative confusion with which the courts have to deal is more than negligible. But, where the fields actually overlap, I see a welter of contradictions as the inevitable consequence.

Of course, these problems will not arise if Scotland, Ulster, and Wales remain directly governed from Westminster. But I do not think they will, and, if they do not, I do not see any hope of legislation passing, or, if it passes, making sense which does not possess the following characteristics. In the first place the powers of the assemblies must not merely be defined and limited by law to certain fields. They must also be limited so as to render invalid any legislation even within the fields devolved which either infringes the rights of individual citizens of Common Market countries, or any human rights inconsistent with the European Convention, or which discriminates against citizens resident in other parts of the United Kingdom. Even if we go no further this will give our constitution many of the characteristics of a 'written' constitution so far as regards the powers of the assemblies. But, quite apart from this, it seems to me essential that the validity of particular enactments of the central Parliament in Westminster must also be open to challenge in the courts by individual litigants or by the executives of the provincial assemblies, if these are to be given the autonomy and sense of responsibility which alone will satisfy the demands of those who want them. In other words if devolution comes, it will have to approximate to federalism in order to be workable. Once this is achieved in this vital field our constitution will cease to be 'unwritten'.

There remains a final argument without which this part of the case would be incomplete. This is the danger to which I have already referred of takeover, to which we shall continue to be exposed so long as we adhere to a constitution of the 'unwritten' or 'uncontrolled' variety.

I am not one to see reds under every bed. But it would be wrong to ignore the fact that it is part of the avowed strategy of the Communist Party of Great Britain, and part of the implicit strategy of all militant leftist or rightist groups to use the power of Parliament to communize the country, or, as the case may be to make it conform to some other authoritarian model. So far as concerns right-wing groups, this was very clearly defined in Sir Oswald Mosley's pre-war utterances, and, although it may not yet be clearly defined, it would in my judgement be quite impossible for a body like the National Front to carry out its avowed programme without passing through Parliament legislation which would breach any rational constitution of the 'written' variety.

So long as there is no effective second chamber, and our voting system remains of the 'first past the post' variety our constitution must be particularly vulnerable to a takeover by extremist parties. Indeed, if I have correctly understood the doctrine avowed by the Communist Party of Great Britain in 'The British Road to Socialism', a takeover of this kind, coupled with a similar manipulation of the unions and other bodies, must be implicit in the denial that civil war or violent revolution are necessary to the attainment of their aims. Obviously reforms in the nature of the second chamber, and of other kinds I have recommended, would make such a takeover less easy. But surely we should need our heads examined if we did not further entrench our laws and liberties, and our institutions by a constitution 'written' or 'controlled' in all the ways I have sought to describe.

XXII

THE QUEEN

The first and most decorative of our institutions is the monarchy. No one, at least no one who has seen the great royal occasions, the Coronation, the opening of Parliament, even the trooping of the Colour, will object to my use of the word 'decorative'. My purpose, however, is to discuss its utility and not the aesthetic beauty of its ceremonies.

I must immediately make a qualification. When late in life, I first visited India, I made, of course, the customary pilgrimage to Agra to see the Taj Mahal. A rather intrusive Canadian member of the party began to bewail its lack of utilitarian value. I was slightly irritated. 'It is possible to argue,' I replied somewhat pompously, 'that beauty itself serves some useful purpose.'

In a free society the subject matter of politics is debate, and debate is about the matters which divide us. Where there is unanimity there can be no debate, and no politics. Talk of a government of national unity, or an end to party bickering is either tantamount to a proclamation of a state of war, or to a demand for a dictatorship.

But, as I have tried to argue, a nation cannot exist without unity. It cannot survive on its divisions alone. It needs cement. It requires symbols, or a rallying point, an object of general respect and regard. Our symbol is the Crown. Without that symbol we should fall apart, that is unless or until a new symbol could be found. The value of the symbol is enhanced by its beauty, its venerable antiquity, and the warmth and colour of the emotional family life which its very nature can and does provide. The cement binding a nation's spirit together consists partly of common needs and interests, but also upon shared values and traditions. The Crown symbolizes our present need for unity which in its turn derives from a shared history and shared values. The fact that the Crown is worn by one of ourselves, a vulnerable human being with human anxieties and a mortal end, forms no small part of its value and gives the symbol added poignancy and human interest. The fact that the institution is also hereditary is in itself a guarantee against an undesirable elitism. When in addition its occupant is a warm-hearted and beautiful woman, that is an added bonus.

It is the need for the Crown to be the symbol of unity which has led to the requirement of political impartiality. Among royalists and monarchists from abroad this is seen as an anomaly. But a head of state who is going to rule as well as reign must either be elected from time to time, as is the American President, or assassinated from time to time, as were the Roman emperors. The institution of a hereditary monarchy cannot survive indefinitely once it becomes a matter of party politics.

It is this which makes the defence of the monarchy a peculiarly difficult matter. I am, of course, a dedicated party politician. This means that it is extremely dangerous to the monarchy to receive too many bouquets at my hands, and, for this reason only, I shall try to avoid bestowing them. But I do not pretend to be impartial. I am a passionate believer in our system, and, like most of the senior ministers of all parties who have come into contact with the Queen and other members of the Royal Family, a sincere admirer personally of them and their performance of their duties.

In this chapter, however, I am simply concerned with constitutional mechanisms, and the point I am making is that, quite apart from the value of the sovereign and the Royal Family as symbols of national unity, they have additional political and constitutional functions which are valuable almost in proportion as they are unnoticed. The parts of a machine work well almost in inverse proportion as they attract attention to themselves. The Queen attracts plenty of attention as a symbol. But her most important working function as part of the machinery of government never attracts attention precisely because it is working exactly as it was designed to do. So long as the Queen is there, the regime which we are asked to obey as the government, has her guarantee that its authority is legitimate. If a dictator or a military junta wished to usurp power it would first have to get rid of the Queen who would be bound to risk her own life in order to protect the constitution.

Although we might have to submit to the superior force of a revolutionary regime we should know at least that it was not legitimate. The one way in which a revolutionary regime could install itself without abolishing the monarchy would be if it first captured a majority in Parliament at a general election, and then proceeded to pass laws to preserve its own existence or subjugate the majority under the authority of the Royal Assent. It might be able to achieve this for a time by deceiving the palace advisers of the Crown. But the very difficulty of doing so would be a very powerful deterrent, and, if it succeeded in doing so for any length of time it would certainly destroy the monarchy or at least the occupant of the throne. It was the failure of the Italian King to withdraw before it was too late royal support from the tyranny of Mussolini which destroyed the Italian monarchy. It is not altogether without significance, especially in view of this fact, that it was the dismissal of Mussolini by the King, too late though it was to save his throne, which ultimately destroyed Mussolini.

I was recently asked to participate in a broadcast interview on the monarchy chaired by David Dimbleby, at which I found myself being asked questions about the residual functions of the monarch in which she actually might have to take controversial decisions of her own that might bring the monarchy into question.

This is, of course, not wholly imaginary. The recent Australian crisis during which Sir John Kerr dismissed Mr Whitlam was responsible for a good deal of criticism of the office of Governor General, and even of the monarchy, in Australia. So far as it involved the Queen, the criticism was manifestly absurd, since the appointment by the Queen of Sir John Kerr was on the advice of her Australian ministers, that is to say, Mr Whitlam himself. So far, however, as it was criticism of the office of Governor General it is worth while studying in case there may be lessons which it might offer here.

The particular crisis which led to Mr Whitlam's dismissal could not in fact have occurred in Britain. It occurred because the Australian Senate refused to vote the supply required by the Lower House. This they could do, but the British House of Lords could not. As I am recommending constitutional change which would involve replacing the House of Lords, it is here right that I should say explicitly that, whatever other changes we make, it would be quite wrong to create a second chamber with any right to interfere with supply so as to challenge that of the House of Commons. This is a lesson finally established here by the events of 1909 and which ought to have been obvious for centuries before that, because it was implicit by the form and procedure by which financial legislation had always been passed.

Nor, for reasons which are more complicated but essentially similar, would it be right to interfere with the convention, which for practical purposes has the force of law, by which the political colour of the government of the day is determined by its ability to command a majority in the House of Commons. As Mr Callaghan observed shortly after his return from America, the business of governing is one thing, and that of legislating to change the country's laws is another. One of the defects of our system of government in recent years has been our assumption that the two things are the same. We assume that the mere fact that a party succeeds in achieving a narrow majority in the House of Commons of itself entitles it not merely to form an administration and present a budget but also to push through legislation of all kinds regardless of opposition and criticism, at least, if justification for doing so can be found within the terms of the majority party's election manifesto. This heresy contains at least three errors. The first is to assume that Parliamentary government consists in dictatorship by the majority in the House of Commons and that to pass legislation a government is not obliged to justify itself in debate. The second is to forget that a government may have to act in the public interest even against its own election promises. The third, and cardinal, error is to confuse the executive and legislative functions of government. One of the great needs of the present time is to disentangle the legitimate requirements of executive government from the business of general legislation.

Given, however, these limitations, I was able to assure David Dimbleby that in its remaining constitutional prerogatives the powers of the monarchy are protected by a fail-safe mechanism. All the main parties in the state now select their own leaders, which safeguards the sovereign against the embarrassment of having to choose between individuals as such, as she had to do in 1963. Even at that time, however, the fail-safe mechanism would have operated in the Queen's favour. The test would have been whether the alternative choice, had it been made, would have commanded a majority in the House of Commons. If it would, the monarch would have escaped criticism as she did after the selection of Lord Home. If it would not, an alternative selection would have been necessary until an acceptable leadership had been established.

It is true, of course, that a more difficult situation may occur when the choice is not between individuals as such, but between the leaders representing party groups. But here again the fail-safe mechanism can be seen to operate. Let us suppose that there is no one party in the House of Commons which can command a vote of confidence after a general election. The monarch sends, let us say, for the leader of the largest party. He (I include 'she') forms a government and either fails to get a vote of confidence, in which case an alternative selection is necessary, or either by reason of coalition, acquiescence of the other parties, or an arrangement falling short of coalition, succeeds in getting a majority in which case the selection is justified. An example of this is seen in the crisis of 1931 when, failing to get the support of his colleagues, Ramsay MacDonald offered his resignation, and George V asked him to stay on and form a multi-party government. This he did and the choice was justified by support in the existing House of Commons and endorsement by the country at an election afterwards. Had either decision gone the other way another selection would have been necessary. Of course, a monarch operating this system may make errors, but so long as he or she does not seek to manipulate the system to secure personal power, and so long as the ultimate decision to resolve disputes rests with the electorate, it is difficult to see that a conscientious monarch would not be protected by the fail-safe mechanism.

Far more likely in principle to cause constitutional argument than the power to summon ministers is the power were the situation to occur to refuse a dissolution to a Prime Minister actually in office. So far as I know, this has never happened in Britain in the past hundred years though there was an incident of this kind in Canada just after the First World War. One can just conceive of circumstances in which a Prime Minister asked for a dissolution immediately after a general election and was refused it on the ground that it was premature. But here again a fail-safe mechanism exists. The disappointed Prime Minister would of course resign and state his reasons. The monarch would then have to seek another principal adviser. If none was forthcoming, or none received the necessary vote of confidence, resort would have to be had to the first, and this time the advice would have to be taken. The sovereign would have received a rebuff, but not a final defeat, since the House of Commons and thereafter the electorate would again have been allowed to exercise the final arbitrament.

As I have said, the Australian situation could not repeat itself in Britain in an identical form. In theory, of course, a Prime Minister could refuse to resign or to advise a dissolution when effectively dismissed by the House of Commons, but to say that the Crown might then be under a duty to dismiss him is no more than to say that Prime Ministers are dependent on the confidence of the House of Commons, and that the sovereign, as the ultimate guarantor and trustee of the constitution, must ensure that Prime Ministers must observe the constitution no less than monarchs. If the ensuing general election provided a majority for the recalcitrant Prime Minister he would have recovered legitimacy. If it did not, someone else would have to be selected to give effect to the electoral verdict.

To see the advantages of our present monarchy it is only necessary to compare, and analyse, the alternatives. Apart from authoritiarian regimes, which I will not discuss, there are really only two available alternatives. The first, is the presidential system as practised in the United States or the present republic in France. The second depends on the cabinet system of government with a titular head of state. Examples of this were the Third Republic in France, the Federal Republic in Germany or Ireland. Each has advantages and disadvantages. To my mind neither of the two alternatives bears comparison with our own traditional monarchy. The presidential system as practised in America

XXIII

THE HOUSE OF LORDS

The House of Lords is not elected. It is partly nominated (Law Lords, Bishops, Life Peers, Peers of first creation) and partly hereditary. Individual peers have the status of individual counsellors of the Crown. But it is evident that however responsible, eminent, and wise its members may be, such a body, so composed, has not the moral and political authority necessary to challenge the will of a representative assembly chosen as the result of universal suffrage however inefficient or unsatisfactory the method of election, or however unreasonable the members of the majority groups may be.

One may ask the question how such a body has survived into the latter part of the twentieth century as a separate element in a sovereign legislature. The answer is a peculiar one. It has been preserved because the House of Commons deliberately wished to preserve it in that condition. For a long time, the House of Commons has been uneasily aware that people would not tolerate a sovereign legislature with unlimited powers of which it was itself the only organ. It has, therefore, deliberately kept in being a second chamber of composition so unjustifiable in principle that it could act as a sort of chaperon to the House of Commons without actually challenging its authority. But, over the last ten years, the situation has become increasingly intolerable, at least for members of the House of Lords. Again and again the House of Lords has sought to intervene to restrain the excesses of the ministerial majority in the House of Commons. Again and again they have been proved right, which is not surprising, since the accumulated wisdom of members of the House of Lords, and the level of discussion within the chamber, are infinitely higher than in the Commons. The calibre of members of the House of Lords, and their experience of public life and public affairs generally are superior. The conduct of debate is infinitely more orderly and courteous. Nevertheless, with the exception of a number of important, but relatively minor instances, the House of Lords has been frustrated again and again in its legitimate desire to perform its constitutional duty.

It is, of course, still true that the House of Lords commands a Conservative majority, though this majority has been much eroded of recent years by increased numbers of Labour peers, the solid phalanx of Bishops, and considerable numbers of active and able Liberal peers and cross benchers. The large Conservative majority remains an embarrassment to the Conservative leadership, and various suggestions have been made to mitigate the evil. Whatever else it does, however, it presents no significant threat to, and exercises no effective control over, a Labour majority in the House of Commons.

It is not true that the House of Lords only intervenes against Labour Governments. When a Conservative Government is in power a small number of Conservative peers can easily defeat the government when they vote, as they frequently do, in concert with the Bishops, the Liberals or the Labour benches. The difference is that a successful revolt by the peers, actual, or even threatened when a Conservative Government is in office is almost always successful, because it is unusual for a Conservative Government to challenge a coalition consisting not merely of their opponents but a number of their own supporters, whereas when a Labour Government is defeated in the Lords in a matter to which ministers attach importance, it is usually quite easy for them to override the Lords by using their majority in the Commons and poking fun at the 'unelected chamber'. Only in the rarest cases has it been necessary for a Labour Government to invoke the Parliament Act, and only in one case, when it has done so, has it failed to secure its object, and that was because the government had failed to recognize or had decided to defy the rules regarding hybridity. But, whether a Conservative or a Labour Government is in office, the weakness of the Lords is that it is able to do too little and not that it is able to do too much. It is not able to vindicate the wishes of the people against the government of the day, or even against the bureaucracy and this, in a Parliament of unlimited powers, is precisely what an effective second chamber ought to be in a position to do.

If we may translate my generalizations into the experience of the last ten years, I believe that if a really representative second chamber had existed, the Conservative Government under Mr Heath would have failed to secure unaltered the passage of its Industrial Relations Act, its Local Government Acts in Scotland, England, or Wales, and very likely other important legislative proposals as well. The Labour Governments would not have got through their nationalization measures, the iniquitous bill relieving retrospectively councillors liable to surcharge for deliberate defiance of the law from their liabilities, some at least of the provisions of their trade union legislation, their legislation on agricultural tenancies, and a number of other measures. I leave it to be judged whether this net result would have been desirable or otherwise, but I cannot help thinking myself, that on balance it would.

Personally, I have no real objection to minority governments, that is, governments with a party majority in the House of Commons, but representing a minority of the electorate, and therefore I do not wholly share the view of those who so passionately advocate electoral reform in the Commons. But executive government is one thing, and the right to legislate is another. General legislature should be representative of public opinion. The right to executive government carries with it the right to financial and economic control, and the control of the Civil Service. These should depend on the majority in the Commons. Experience in the last ten years has shown it to be utterly intolerable that it should also carry with it the right of unlimited powers to change the laws of the land. This should be subject to the right of veto of a proportionately elected assembly chosen by universal suffrage.

Various attempts have been made since the makeshift legislation of 1911 (not improved by the equally makeshift amendments of 1949) to introduce compromise proposals designed to make the composition of the House of Lords more acceptable to the electorate. All have foundered for two reasons, each conclusive in its own sphere. The first is that it is simply not theoretically possible to make either a nominated membership or a hereditary membership compatible with the principles of democracy. The second is that the House of Commons is not prepared to share effective power with any chamber which is partly nominated and partly hereditary, or partly ex-officio, partly nominated, and partly hereditary, however the proportions or methods of selection may be juggled about. This is not in any way to criticize the existing House of Lords, least of all its hereditary element, which in my experience contributes a desirable element of common sense, and occasionally, an acceptable element of independence, into an assembly of persons whose members are sometimes lacking at least in the first. It is simply to say that the alternative to radical reform is to maintain the status quo more or less as it is, and, if I am right in describing the status quo as intolerable, there is no genuine alternative to radical reform.

Fortunately, the matter is no longer capable of argument. Sooner or later the Labour Party is going to abolish the status quo. The more radical and foolish wish to go in for a single chamber government with the House of Lords no longer in existence at all and no replacement having been made, the House of Commons would then be left without its chaperon. The wiser, but far more dangerous, proposal would be to leave the anomalous assembly as it is, but further emasculate its powers. An even sillier proposal by the Labour peers is to render it a positive replica of the House of Commons by making membership of it dependent on approval by a select committee of MPs. These would be worse than outright abolition since it would retain a façade of a two-chamber legislature, while concealing the reality of elective dictatorship by one. Outright abolition would at least force Conservatives and Liberals to devise a replacement when the reality of elective dictatorship became obvious. But, in either case, the present House of Lords is doomed, and there is therefore no longer any point in arguing whether or not it should be retained.

The only question is, with what to replace it and when. To my mind there is no alternative to an elected chamber. It must not be elected on the same constituencies, or by the same voting method as the Commons, as a mere mirror image of the Commons would be valueless. Some method of proportional representation is desirable, since the function of a second chamber is to legislate, and to restrain legislation not acceptable to majority opinion. It is no part of its function to act as a Court of Appeal from the verdict of the people, and therefore, legislation should pass through when it is proposed, or amended in a form acceptable to the majority. The method of proportional representation, is, of course, for discussion. My own preference would be for very large constituencies, Scotland, Wales, Northern Ireland, the Midlands, the West, the North-West, the North-East, the South-East, the South, and party lists, including a list of independents which might include some of the religious leaders. Other systems would be acceptable. My own preference would be for this body to be elected at the same time as the Commons. This would minimize the extent of the clash between the two Houses, and enable any kind of conflict to be resolved by dissolution. Others, more conservatively minded than myself, might prefer election for a fixed term and retirement by rotation, as with the American Senate and some local authorities.

The powers of the second chamber to restrain the government would be limited to legislation and statutory instruments. The political colour of the executive and control of finance and economic policy, would remain with government, as at present, so long as it retained a majority in the Commons. The new second chamber would act as a brake to prevent contentious legislation which had no real basis of popular approval, and insist on improvements on legislation which contained excessive or unreasonable features. I would hope that its procedures and operation would be modelled on those of the existing House of Lords, and that many of its first members would be existing peers. I would hope that it would continue to be presided over by the Lord Chancellor of the day. It would be a question for consideration whether the nine or ten nominated law lords should continue, as now, to discharge the functions of the ultimate Court of Appeal, or whether the same gentlemen should move over to Downing Street and their appellate powers transferred to the Judicial Committee of the Privy Council. It would make no difference to the actual result of cases which alternative were adopted, though I myself prefer the procedure in the House of Lords, with separate opinions delivered, to the corporate advice contained in a Privy Council judgement. The main point is to restore genuine bicameralism to the United Kingdom legislature, and to base those powers on universal suffrage and proportional representation. This can be done only by creating, as the Parliament Act originally proposed, an elective second chamber which would possess real authority as the people's representatives and not the embarrassment of a built-in Conservative majority or a membership derived partly from nomination or appointment, and partly from hereditary honours.

XXIV

THE GOVERNMENT MACHINE

At the heart of the elective dictatorship resides the government machine, the bureaucracy, the Civil Service. Almost entirely, the functions and working of this intricate mechanism, perhaps the most perfect, efficient and disinterested the world has ever seen, is the product of convention, tradition, and administrative practice. It is hardly known to the formal legal theory of the constitution. From the earliest days Queen, Lords and Commons have been familiar names. They are indissolubly part of the legal theory of the state. So is the Privy Council, the old organ of Tudor administration, still surviving as a formalized piece of legal machinery operating in the presence of the sovereign, at which nothing serious is ever discussed, and in its Judicial Committee as a court of law sitting in Downing Street. Individual ministers have a definite legal being, either as the creations of statute or as the result of the extension of the functions of the ancient office of Secretary of State. Constitutionally speaking, the Cabinet is simply a meeting of the Queen's servants sitting in private as an informal gathering of Privy Councillors, under the Chairmanship of Her Majesty's principal Minister, until recently operating only as First Lord of the Treasury, one of the Lords holding jointly the old office of Lord High Treasurer which had been found, like the Lord High Admiral, to be too powerful a position to be held by a single subject. The real government machine, its operative parts, its personnel, its committees, its agenda, its conclusions, its ethos, its traditions, is shrouded in mystery, its deliberations secretively concealed behind the legal fiction, except in so far as corners of the veil are coyly lifted during debates of the House of Commons.

I am not one of those, like Richard Crossman, who at any time entertained doubts of the integrity, the industry, the impartiality or the efficiency of the government machine. I would be the first to denounce the conspiratorial theory occasionally promulgated by less well-informed Labour supporters. The Civil Service is, in fact, all that its most ardent supporters crack it up to be, like the Brigade of Guards, the Bank of England, the judiciary, and many other typically British institutions. But it is very close to the seat of power, and because of the eclipse of Britain, its influence must be closely studied, for, despite its many virtues, its operations must bear some of the responsibility for what has been happening in the past thirty years.

Except for the Law Officers of the Crown, and the Lord Chancellor, Cabinet government is largely a government by amateurs, mediated and translated into action by professionals. This is probably true to some extent in all democracies. The amateur factor is far more prominent in the USA when a change of Presidency introduces into the executive government a whole new coterie of inexperienced, if brilliant, amateur enthusiasts, vulnerable to flattery, capable of corruption, liable to incredible mistakes and ultimately guided and controlled by the will of a President whose sole experience in national or international affairs prior to election may have been a seat in the Senate or a State Governorship.

By comparison, Britain's Cabinet Ministers are experts. Few achieve Cabinet rank from the outside without years of apprenticeship in one House of Parliament and usually some experience of subordinate office. But they are amateurs all the same. When I became First Lord of the Admiralty I had never been to sea except as a passenger. When I became Minister of Education, I had no experience of education except as a pupil and none of the state schools except as a governor of the Quintin Grammar School.

The same is true of almost every minister I have ever known. Our sole title to govern is based on the result of a general election giving our party a majority in the House of Commons, and our main qualification for office is our real or presumed capacity to persuade the House of Commons, or possibly the House of Lords, to accept or at least acquiesce in the decisions to which we have come. Our wisdom in council operates marginally in our favour when we have acquired experience. Our quality as administrators usually becomes known, principally to the Prime Minister, through the Civil Service grapevine. We frequently find ourselves overborne in our judgement by the intransigence or stupidity of colleagues or other departments, or the exigencies of some financial edict. Particularly, in our frequent crises, we find ourselves blamed for meanness or hardness of heart, when what has really happened is that our strenuous efforts to promote the interests of our department, or the needs which it exists to satisfy, have been defeated by some alliance between the Treasury and rival claimants to its largesse. We seldom stay long enough in a particular office to see the fruits, good or bad, of our more important decisions.

By contrast we often have to bear the blame, or sometimes even to enjoy the praise, due in reality to one of our predecessors, not infrequently of the opposite party. To support us in this strange game of rewards and forfeits the conventions of government compel us to adopt the ethics of the private school, or even the thieves' kitchen. These, by no means bad rules of thumb for the conduct of life in this wicked world, principally consist in two commandments, namely these: Thou shalt not blub, and thou shalt not sneak. I am not myself a critic of these traditions, though in origin they are comparatively modern. They have enabled the United Kingdom and, for a time, the British Empire, to survive two world wars, and to preside over the fortunes of our most successful political community.

At the moment, however, I am concerned with shortcomings rather than panegyric. There is as great a gulf fixed between those in Parliament who have not, and those who have, experience of office, as between those who have, and those who have not passed through Caterham Barracks, or Dartmouth, or a theological seminary, as between a professor and an undergraduate in his first term, as between a judge and a newly called barrister. The difference is increased rather than diminished by the secrecy surrounding the conventions and the actual machinery of government. The gulf accentuates the loneliness of office, but it vastly increases the power and influence of the office holders.

The structure of the machine is held together by the administrative class of the Civil Service (I include the Foreign Service in the expression), surely one of the most talented bodies of men ever to be engaged in the art and science of civil government, recruited from the cream of the universities, selected by examination and interview, trained in political impartiality and secretiveness, rewarded for industry far beyond the calls of duty, advanced for efficiency, and gaining during the experience of a working lifetime more than the most able and experienced minister can summon to his task. Of all political administrators they are most like the class of guardians in Plato's republic, in all things save one. Unlike those guardians, they do not openly bear responsibility for what is done. That must be borne by the minister whom they tend and feed, and strip of the necessary decisions as the worker bees in the hive tend and strip the queen of her eggs as she is led with docility round the cells.

The administrative class of the Civil Service is a relatively modern institution, dating from the reign of Queen Victoria, when it took over from the less efficient system of patronage and corruption native to this island. It is not difficult to divine its origin. It is not the product of Parliamentary government, nor yet of democracy. It came from Imperial China, and though it may at first seem surprising that an institution so alien and so remote landed up on our shores, the paradox becomes less acute when we remember that it was transmitted hither from British India where the fertile genius of Lord Macaulay had introduced it, examinations in the classics and all, from the land of its birth together with the cultivation of silk and the discovery of the native tea plant from Assam.

Any attack on the Civil Service must take account of the immense virtues and integrity of the civil servants. That is where Crossman, and the far less talented Joe Haines, go wrong. Without the administrative class of the Civil Service, our top-heavy, overcentralized, and excessively intrusive system of bureaucracy would have broken down long ago or have developed into an intolerable tyranny on Fascist or quasi-Communist lines. It is due to them, and not to the system, that British government has remained reasonably sane, tolerably just, and in comparison with local government and foreign countries, almost impeccably incorrupt. That does not mean that the system is intrinsically sound, or that it should be allowed to continue unaltered.

The administrative class of the Civil Service is the main
source of what comes across the minister's table from the
day when he first enters the minister's office to the day when
he leaves it suitably swept and garnished and ready for its
next occupant. It is wholly wrong to suggest that senior
civil servants are in the least biased in the material they
place before their minister. It is simply true to say that what
comes, when it comes, and the form in which it is delivered,
is determined in practice almost entirely by this talented and
highly disciplined force. The minister exercises his judgement,
if he is an honest and intelligent man, impeccably. But after
a bit he comes to realize, that almost any honest and intelligent man of equal ability would have been bound to
come to the same conclusion had he been fed with the same
information. He is not given the full force of the acute
controversy which has sometimes been going on within the
department, and he is not infrequently so impregnated with
the view held within his department where it is unanimous
that he finds it difficult to believe in controversy with his
colleagues, who have been similarly briefed by their own
civil servants, that they are not being actively dishonest or
stupid in arguing for a different conclusion.

In Parliamentary controversy the minister, however mis-
guided, has a devoted and loyal team to brief him to defend
his decisions, or rather the decisions and events for which he
is responsible, against criticism in the House, either from
the opposition or from within his own party. So convincing
are these briefs that the minister must often get away with it
even where he is wrong, especially if he is himself endowed
with debating skills, or the techniques and qualifications of
forensic advocacy. He only finds it a snare and a delusion
when he is faced with an emotional storm which no Parliamentary performance can quell, or on the rare occasions
when the brief is broken down by unusual skills or the rarely
acquired effective brief on the opposition side. He may, in
the end, be the victim of his own shortcomings, intellectual
arrogance, irascibility, or insensitiveness to a Parliamentary
atmosphere. But he starts with an initial advantage over his
opponents which is more than the intrinsic merits of his
case always deserve. Since in the majority of cases his
audience in the House of Commons consists of a majority of

members of his own party longing to see him score a triumph over the forces of opposition, or where he is dealing with internal opposition, of critics who have been softened up by the party whips or neutralized by deliberately solicited back-bench speeches on the minister's side, the task even of an inexpert minister is often easier than might be expected.

The combined result of ministerial control of the government machine and the possession of a Parliamentary majority adds immense force to the power of modern government. This power is vastly increased by the immense volume of work passing through Parliament at any given moment of time, the small resources in time, money or assistance available to back benchers or opposition for research, and the various devices open to government to curtail debate by the use of closure and guillotine, and the necessary, if impartial, power of selection given to the Chair to select speakers and discriminate between amendments.

It is not possible to argue that this is an ideal system of government. In my opinion it is a major factor in the increasing remoteness of government from the people. We have the most highly centralized administration in the free world. We are in fact governed by a bureaucracy of mandarins and their subordinates imposing on a people partisan policies devised by a government of amateurs who have achieved their position by a minority of votes under an unfair voting system, bringing into Parliament candidates selected by local caucuses of activists or outside bodes and having little else to commend them but their party loyalties. The miracle of it is that it does not work as badly in practice as it ought to do. That it does not do so is largely due to the character of the British people and the talents of its public servants. It is, however, at least for consideration whether a more highly devolved, less overworked, and more limited system of government would not serve better the purposes of today.

Those who have identified some of the shortcomings I have attempted to describe come forward with various types of remedy, the political adviser whose function it is to weaken the control of the Civil Service by keeping the minister more strictly to the party line, a greater degree of transferability between Civil Service and industry, with later intakes and temporary appointments, a less stringent entry qualification to allow for a wider social background. I am not of their number. Given our system of government, I am prepared to go to the stake against any attempt to water down or undermine the quality, the morale, the discipline, or the independence of our administrative civil servants. They do their best to mitigate the system's faults, whereas the various remedies proposed would exaggerate the faults they are supposed to remedy. It is the system itself that I call in question.

The highly organized and centralized bureaucracy necessary to operate our system of government over a population of more than 60 millions is an evil only because the system of government itself is defective. It was tolerable, even beneficial, in former days precisely because central government controlled so small a portion of our lives. Now that in almost every field of activity, government intrudes, it needs to be broken down into smaller units with divided power. Now that party politics and party loyalties play such a predominant role in legislative policy, the powers of Parliament need to be controlled. The Civil Service is an evil at present, not because of its vices, but because of its virtues, not because it is not impartial, but because it adds to the power of the elective dictators, according impartially its skills, its disciplines, its expertise to the organized minority in power so that it becomes less possible to unseat them. The fact that it feeds ministers with predigested information does indeed limit their choice, but, on balance, it saves them from ideological aberrations and errors of judgement. The weaknesses of our system of government consist in an omnipotent House of Commons, an overcentralized executive, and too weak and shackled a judiciary. The excellence of the administrative Civil Service is not one of these weaknesses. But it does strengthen the hold of the elective dictatorship, and its presence, while mitigating some of its faults, helps to mask some of its deficiencies.

XXV

NATIONALISM AND DEVOLUTION

I learned my first political lessons before World War I. I was taught to believe in the unity of the British Isles, and that my own family was Irish on my father's side. Indeed, when my great grandfather approached his prospective father-in-law (who was English) with a view to marrying his daughter, family tradition says he was dismissed at first with the words: 'Go away, you impudent young Irishman.' My uncle, Ian Hogg, one of the first casualties in the First World War, then commanding the 4th Hussars, was stationed in the Curragh at the time of the famous 'incident', and even now his part in it appears in some of the more detailed historical accounts of the episode. My wife's family lived in County Galway from the time of Strongbow to the Treaty.

There is now no Irish people. There are two. There are those north or south of the border who own allegiance to the Republic. Two-thirds of the Protestant minority, in what is now the Republic, has now left the south. It has voted with its feet. In the north there is a separate Protestant majority bound devotedly to the Union and with even greater enthusiasm wishing neither part nor lot with the people of the Republic.

I have never been hostile to Irish nationalism. But I still believe in the unity of the British Isles. I believe that the failure of the United Kingdom in the nineteenth century and before the Treaty to come to terms with Irish nationalism by way of federation or devolution has been the cause of many evils to Ireland, to the rest of Britain, and to the rest of the world. There have always been those who claim that if the Coalition in 1921 had been firm with Sinn Fein or even shot De Valera at the time of the Easter Rising, Irish nationalism would have gone away and hid. There are others who believe that separation should have been granted from the first. I belong to neither school. I am prepared to admit that there were things wrong with all our Home Rule

Bills and Acts which would have justified a cantankerous or nit-picking opposition in voting against them on second reading. But I believe that one or more of them should have been tried, and if this had been attempted in time, it is at least possible that we should now have a federal United Kingdom of Great Britain and Ireland, and that we should have peace, absolute or relative, in Ulster today.

There is no going back on past mistakes. But it seems to me that there is no reason to repeat them. When I see the growth of Scottish nationalism and Welsh nationalism, I believe without doubting that the result of these movements, if successful, would lead to a repetition of all the evils inherent in what has happened in Ireland. There is no Irish nation today. There are two communities, even in the south, but, of course, more particularly in the north, that which clings to Britishness and that which urges its Irishness. Both are profoundly unhappy and each adds to the unhappiness of the other. But to see in the island of Britain two Scottish peoples, and two Welsh peoples, one asserting its Scottishness or its Welshness, and one, whether a minority or a majority, clinging to its Britishness (which involves association with England) would be a tragedy for all of us beyond tears or hope of remedy. If Walloons and Flemings can form one Belgium, or if Schwyzer Dütsch, Suisses Romands, and Ticinesi can form one Switzerland, if Allemanisch-speaking Alsace can be part of France, and French-speaking Breuil or German-speaking Bolzano part of Italy, I can see no reason why the United Kingdom cannot remain united, provided of course that people are willing to make reasonable adjustments.

Before the Act of Union, Britain was an island without vast importance in the scheme of things. The glories of Elizabethan England (after Flodden) are admitted. But the Britain which has since conquered the seas, developed an empire and dismantled it, resisted successive European tyrannies, founded new nations, given laws to continents, pioneered science and industry and sport, Britain in short as we know it hardly existed until the Act of Union. Even after the Union of the two Crowns Britain was a geographical expression but not a nation. Why should we now turn our back on the past and allow ourselves to be converted back into three or four little independent states each played off against the other by commercial and political rivals, the whole totally unable to defend itself, and resting, for defence, on European and American bayonets and missiles? The folly and short-sightedness of it leaves me aghast. Of course Norway and Denmark, Switzerland and Sweden, Luxembourg, Holland, Belgium exist independently (up to a point) on a scale equal or greater than the several parts of the British Isles. But how, or why? Is it not because of the blood shed in streams by British men and women from all parts of the United Kingdom in two world wars? Without this they would be fiefs of the Greater Reich, which, for aught we know, might well have lasted, as its champions predicted, in all its horror for a thousand years.

Of course if Scottish nationalism would just go away I would be well enough pleased to retain the status quo. There are English and Scots who believe that, given a firm 'no', it will go away, and that Welsh nationalism will never really get off the ground. There are also Scots Conservatives who, cannily enough, observe that an independent Scotland would be governed by the industrial belt round Glasgow, and would prefer domination by Westminster to domination by Socialist Scots. Even though England would become indelibly Conservative I can sympathize with that. But if Scottish nationalism will not just go away, the time must come when it will predominate, at least for long enough to secede. Governments of all kinds become unpopular, and the nationalist feelings which have always existed in Scotland and Wales will eventually get out of hand. If it were simply a question of preserving Conservative Scots from a Socialist philosophy preferred over a period by a majority of Scots voters there would be little to say against the nationalist case.

But will Scots nationalism go away? Is it just a temporary aberration like the student troubles of the 1960s, a sort of political hiccup, which will disappear if you take a deep breath and pretend it is not there? This is the question which must be answered before an answer can be found to the question which next arises, that is, how Scotland should be governed. This is the second question. But there is a third which arises after that, if the answer to the first two involves a change of status to Scotland. The third question is this. If we are to assume that a change of status to Scotland is necessary, what are the changes which will follow in the other parts of the now disunited kingdom of England, Scotland, Wales and Northern Ireland, and, even for that matter, the Channel Isles and the Isle of Man? I regard it as fanciful to suppose that there will be none, or that none will prove desirable.

Obviously the question whether Scottish nationalism will just go away is a matter for personal assessment. In the nature of things, the answer, affirmative or not, is intrinsically incapable of proof. But my own assessment is that it will not. I do not pretend that I am not influenced by subjective impressions received during visits to Scotland and by talk with Scottish Nationalist MPs. If these stood alone I would not myself ask that I should be listened to. But they do not stand alone.

I have been trying to paint a picture of Britain today which exhibits the paradox of elective dictatorship, an over-centralized and top-heavy state, possessing absolute powers in theory, but unable to exercise them in practice, using them oppressively in innumerable small things, but unable to pursue a steady and consistent course in great, a House of Commons elected but unrepresentative, attempting too much work and achieving too few results, arrogant but possessing insufficient authority, a House of Lords which is all but impotent, a bureaucracy which is overcentralized, pressure groups and parties seeking to control the levers of power and succeeding in doing so occasionally, but spasmodically and in inconsistent ways. Above all, I am trying to suggest that, with the increase in the scope and intrusiveness of modern government, the unit of the United Kingdom is far too large to be operated as a unitary state devoid of constitutional safeguards.

Now if the whole, or any part of this, is a fair diagnosis of our present condition, Scottish nationalism will not go away because the grievances to which it gives expression are genuine. Elsewhere, without the spark of national memories, tradition and sentiment, they give rise to different signs, functional and otherwise, of disaffection, pressure groups, demonstrations, splinter parties, disobedience. But the grievances are still there and need to be remedied.

Moreover, in one way Scotland suffers from them more acutely than most and has suffered them longer. The concentration of many departments in the office of a single Secretary of State is an absurd arrangement for a country of seven millions. How can a single man be Minister of Agriculture, Minister of Transport, Minister of Education, Minister of Local Government, and Home Secretary at the same time, and at the same time look after Scottish interests in negotiation with the other departments, not least the Treasury, Employment, the Environment, Foreign Affairs and Defence? The thing is absurd, and should never have been allowed to come to pass. It would never have done so if, after the Act of Union, Scotland had not been left virtually to be governed by the Lord Advocate, who then except in his capacity as Law Officer gave way to the Secretary of State.

The move of the Scottish Office from its place in Whitehall near to the Houses of Parliament and its members to St Andrew's House, was a well-meant gesture intended to gratify national feelings, but was not necessarily an administrative advance. All these factors accentuate the top-heaviness and overcentralization, the bureaucratization and the remoteness from the people of our modern British state. If there were any latent nationalism or separation present in the Scottish soul, this was surely the way to foment it. I make no comment on the claims by nationalists that Scottish interests have been under-represented at Westminster or Scotland exploited. I think these are exaggerated and probably false. But as a way of governing a country of proud traditions and sensitive susceptibilities, as a mere instrument of administration, our present arrangements scarcely bear examination.

For a moment, I will not consider the separate position of Wales. But I now turn my gaze across St George's Channel to Northern Ireland. Here we have another, and rather curious paradox. Let us forget for a moment the intractable communal problem, the two-thirds Protestant to one-third Catholic, the two-thirds West British and one-third Bog Irish, the Lambeg Drums, the Orange Order, the Ancient Order of Hibernians, the Gaelic Athletic Association, the

Old Orange Flute and the Soldier's Song, the celebrations of the Boyne and the Easter Rising, all the ritual and paraphernalia of tribal warfare and communal strife. These occupy the centre of the scene. But, for a moment forgotten, a curious fact emerges. Apart from communal strife, the Government of Ireland Act 1920 worked very well for fifty years in the Six Counties even with a power of local taxation which was little more than minimal. The roads were fine, the agriculture first class, the educational system gave rise to no insuperable problems, relations with Westminster were friendly. The machine, as a machine, worked well, and if it had not been for the constant strife due to the presence of two communities of divided loyalty, and the consequent presence of a permanent one-party government, on the whole it would have been an experiment well worth repeating. The economic troubles of unemployment were not the result of devolution. Apart from communalism, devolution worked and worked well. It exhibited none of the faults visible at Westminster. The tragedy of it was that it came too late to the south to save the Union. If it had been introduced in 1883 I fancy the history of Ireland might well have been different.

I do not pretend that I have been happy with the various proposals of the political parties at Westminster to handle this problem. It seems to me that they fail to cross the necessary logical bridges. Compromise may be a splendidly British virtue, but in constitutional matters issues must be faced. You cannot have a system which is at once federal and unitary. You cannot have local assemblies with jurisdiction concurrent to that of Parliament. I know that in theory this is what occurred at Stormont, but that is partly because the system was operated by conventions observed on both sides as if it were a federation which in fact it was not, and partly because the permanent majority at Stormont was determined to get on with Westminster and the minority largely opted out altogether.

If you have devolution you must actually devolve powers from Westminster, and this means defining frontiers of jurisdiction as in the United States, as in Canada, as in Australia, as in Germany, as in Switzerland between what can be done by the central government and legislature, and what can be done by States, Provinces, Cantons or whatever you choose to call the federated parts. The whole must be policed by the courts, and if you complain that this, up to a point, means political judges, at this stage I simply say that all the countries which I have named appear to get along very well with what is needed, and I rather doubt whether British judges in Scotland, England, Wales, or Northern Ireland are stupider or more biased than those in Georgia, Washington, Ontario, Ottawa, Canberra, Bonn, Berne, or Sydney, or, for that matter Paris, where, although they have not a federal they, at least, have a written constitution.

I leave this subject for the moment with these further comments. The first is that once it is accepted for other reasons that devolution is a good thing, then it helps to answer a great number of other questions. Do we find the House of Commons over-burdened with work and sitting for protracted hours? After devolution, it will have passed over many of the hours and a good deal of the work to other bodies. Doing less it will be able to have fewer members, and that means that there will be less talk and more action. Do we find our central bureaucracy top-heavy and over-burdened and our ministers overworked? The centralized bureaucracy will be split up and shared between different bodies. Under devolution ministers will have less to do. In Scotland the extraordinary office of the Secretary of State, if it continues to exist at all, will be limited to matters like judicial appointments and Scottish law and order. Almost all the other functions of St Andrew's House and the Scottish Office will become separate divisions of authority under the local assembly and its officers.

My second comment is that devolution will compel us to think more deeply about questions of individual legal rights and the limits to be imposed on local legislation. To my mind it is unthinkable that we should allow local assemblies to legislate in such a way as to infringe the rights of individuals guaranteed by international law and subject to the European Court at Brussels or in such a way as to discriminate against EEC nationals or the inhabitants of England or Wales. We shall have to define these rights and make them amenable to the Court of Session in Edinburgh, and, in so far as devolution applies elsewhere, the High

Courts in Belfast and London. If we are to do this, we may as well take the opportunity to define a means by which Acts of Parliament may themselves be amenable to criticism by the courts. In other words we shall have a British Bill of Rights. I shall be discussing the desirability or otherwise of this in the next chapter.

My last observation is that it is, in the end, unthinkable that the terms on which we are to be fellow citizens within a single society should be markedly different according as to whether we live in Belfast, Cardiff, Edinburgh or London. I believe that in the last resort, an assembly in Edinburgh and Belfast would make it impossible to avoid similar assemblies in Wales and England, and since no one wishes to see an English Parliament outside Westminster, these assemblies will have to be regional and, in England, less than national in character. I believe, therefore, that if I am right in predicting the necessity for an assembly in Edinburgh and another in Belfast (so soon as the present troubles are at an end) there will have to be other and similar bodies in Cardiff, and, say, Liverpool, Manchester, Birmingham, Newcastle, Norwich and Bristol, Exeter or Southampton. If we are to come to terms with federalism, it will, I believe, be necessary to do so thoroughly. Why not?

XXVI

A BILL OF RIGHTS

It is the mark, on the whole, of an unsophisticated state of society to lay emphasis on general declarations of right. In early days the declaration by a monarch that to no man he would sell, to no man he would deny or delay justice, was of immediate concern and of immense value. Today, no one supposes that it prevents the government from charging substantial court fees or slipping a substantial duty on the issue of a writ or that it is a guarantee of a speedy trial in an over-congested court.

The principles of impartial justice have passed beyond the stage of general declarations and need to be worked out in detail in an articulated form of modern law. The right to life develops into compensation for death or physical injury in civil procedure and into the law of murder and manslaughter in criminal jurisdiction. The right to liberty would be valueless without habeas corpus or an action for false imprisonment or malicious prosecution. Moreover, since the several rights of individuals are both inconsistent with one another and, at times, with the right of the general public, rhetorically expressed declarations of rights are of little value. They have to be expressed in such qualified language and subject to so many legitimate exceptions that an ill-intentioned government, or even an ingenious individual, would find no difficulty in driving a coach and horse through them. Again and again Bills of Rights have proved an inadequate safeguard against tyranny.

There is also the problem of enumerating the rights considered worthy of inclusion. If one includes the right of association, shall one include the right of non-association, which would exclude the closed shop? If we allow the citizen the right of free speech, does that mean that at election times or even at others he is entitled to wake me up with the distasteful and deafening noise of the loud-speaker van? Is conscription, in war or peace, a breach of fundamental human right? Is defamation consistent with a right of free speech? Is there a fundamental right of privacy and, if so, what are its limits? How far is there a fundamental human right of sexual freedom? To these questions, and to innumerable others, there is really no answer. What is certain is that to establish and entrench them all would be to deny nearly all power to legislatures, and produce almost complete anarchy in all courts.

There is another difficulty in the way of those who wish to live under some form of written British constitution. This is the logical difficulty. Since Parliaments are legally omnipotent, one Parliament can repeal or amend anything a previous Parliament has enacted. It follows that a Bill of Rights, except as a guide to governments setting out a code of good behaviour, may not be worth the paper it is written on. There is no procedure known to the laws of the United Kingdom by which a Parliament can prevent its successors from undoing its work, even as it claims the right to undo the work of its predecessors or reverse the rules of Common Law.

When I was young and reading for the Bar examinations, all this was trite stuff and had few critics among English lawyers. For a time I, too, accepted it as orthodoxy, and there are many lawyers, in Parliament and on the judicial bench, who accept it today. But there is a growing body of opinion which takes an opposite point of view, and, with one qualification, I belong to this camp.

When I was in Mr Macmillan's Government, I visited Canada, and was proudly shown by the Canadian Prime Minister, then Mr Diefenbaker, the draft of what afterwards came to be enacted as the Canadian Bill of Rights. This endeavoured to get round some of these difficulties by enacting a new rule by which Canadian judges were in future to determine the meaning of Acts of Parliament. This was that they should always construe Canadian legislation in a way so as not to breach the rights entrenched in the Bill, unless the legislation expressly stated the contrary. This was Mr Diefenbaker's attempt to reconcile the sovereignty of a Parliament with entrenched rights. At the time, I did not think much of the proposal, partly owing to the vagueness of the rights proposed, and partly because I thought that if a government with a strong majority desired to repeal or amend either the rule of construction, or the Act or both it would not hesitate to do so.

For a time it looked as if the first part of this criticism was sound. For many years, only one case came before the Canadian Courts under the Canadian Bill, when an Indian, with the rather bizarre name of Drybones, claimed the right under it to get drunk outside the Indian Reservation, and won his case. Later, I believe, a quite considerable body of reputable jurisprudence has grown up about the construction of the Canadian Bill, and at least the Bill has in fact remained unaltered on the Canadian statute book. I still have my reservations about its usefulness in the absence of provisions entrenching the rights as part of the Canadian constitution, and limiting the powers of Parliament to encroach upon them. But it has not proved a complete dead letter, and it has now become a settled part of Canadian law.

I have always been less impressed by the difficulties of definition. Both the Universal Declaration of Human Rights of 1948, which imposes only an unenforceable moral obligation, and the European Convention, which is built on it, and which is enforceable by the European Court at Strasbourg, contain valuable declarations, which might well have prevented some recent Acts of Parliament from becoming law had either been part of the domestic law of the United Kingdom. It was the fact that successive governments of the United Kingdom had in fact adhered to the European Convention, including that part of it giving rights of access to the court by individuals which ultimately convinced me of the possible advantage of incorporating the Act into British law. To the argument that it would create a breed of political judges, I reply that whether these rights are incorporated or not, British judges are inevitably involved in decisions having sensitive political consequences. Examples can be found each year and might include among recent decisions the Laker Airways case, the conflict between the Secretary of State and the Tameside Education authority, and recent decisions affecting the powers of the Attorney General, the Post Office, the Water Rates, and the wireless licences. These, which spring to mind at once, are, of course, only a few among many. Secondly, I point to the fact that the European judges at Brussels are already seised of cases involving the government of the United Kingdom, and I simply do not believe that English, Scottish and Northern Irish judges are constitutionally incompetent to deal with the same questions as the European judges.

The argument in fact goes further. Virtually all civilized nations except ourselves, New Zealand, and possibly Israel, have limited constitutions, that is, constitutions in which the powers of the legislature are limited by law and special procedures are necessary to give effect to legislation involving constitutional change. The judges in these countries do not in practice find it beyond their power to exercise coercive jurisdiction over the legislature, and when they do exercise such jurisdiction against alleged excess, whilst their decisions do give rise to controversy, they are by no means always unpopular. The third point is that whatever may be the case in relation to the central legislature, it is virtually inevitable that, in federal countries, the subordinate legislatures have their powers limited by law and excessive use of them restrained by the courts at the instance of local communities, the Federal Government, minorities and private citizens. For these reasons I do not find the argument about political judges conclusive. I might add that in Northern Ireland, some rights of religious minorities were entrenched against Stormont as long ago as 1920, and the courts had no difficulty in enforcing them where necessary. I myself even had difficulty with the Government of Ireland Act while Lord Chancellor when I sought to get a Unionist Attorney General to give special immunities from the general provisions of the health legislation to a Christian Science nursing home. He said that the rule against religious discrimination would prevent a court recognizing such a provision as valid.

Even without entrenchment, a Bill of Rights on the Canadian lines embodying the European Convention would prevent any inadvertent encroachment by Parliament on individual liberties. These encroachments are not by any means so infrequent as might be supposed. The volume of legislation passing through Parliament is now so vast and its complexity so daunting that whole sections and systems sometimes escape scrutiny until the damage is done. Even deliberate invasions of human rights would, at least, be pinpointed if the Canadian system were adopted, and it is at least arguable that a government would be deterred from deliberate encroachment made in the course of legislation only marginally important to them by the necessity to draw attention to the fact that their proposals would or might involve a breach of the Bill.

I would admit, of course, quite candidly that the full benefit of entrenched clauses would only be attainable if the powers of Parliament could, by some means, be limited for the future by providing that constitutional change could only take place by a special procedure, involving some action by a process external to Parliament sanctioning the change. One such means would be a confirmatory referendum. But I would welcome such a course. I wish to put an end to the elective dictatorship. I wish to make it impossible for governments ever again to defy the will of the electorate as they have been doing in recent years by misusing, as I would claim, the unlimited powers of Parliament and insisting on overriding the House of Lords either by the use, actual or threatened, of the Parliament Acts or rejecting particular amendments. From this point of view a Bill of Rights would be a blessing. A constitution of this type would, of course, not be unalterable. There would be procedures for amendment, probably involving a referendum, which could not be interfered with by the courts. There would also be political checks and balances additional to the limitations imposed by law, partly consisting in the installation of subordinate assemblies, and partly by the creation of an effective second chamber. But in this armoury of weapons against elective dictatorship, a Bill of Rights, embodying and entrenching the European Convention might well have a valuable, even if subordinate, part to play.

XXVII

THE EUROPEAN DIMENSION

The existence of the European Convention has an obvious and direct bearing on the desirability of a Bill of Rights. Although it has not yet had to do so, the Strasbourg Court could, at least in theory, condemn not merely the actions of government, but the whole or parts of Acts of Parliament. The European Community has an even more direct bearing on our constitutional arrangements. Like the Strasbourg Court, such decisions would have immediate effect here overriding English law unless they were *ultra vires* the treaty. What is not so generally realized is that, even independently of any such decisions at Luxembourg, the English and Scottish Courts have similar powers and duties, since, in matters in which European law has overriding effect our domestic courts are bound to give effect to it so soon as the fact is brought to their attention. This is the result of the Act of Parliament acceding to the treaty, and, although it would be possible in theory for Parliament to repeal or modify this Act, it would clearly be a breach of the treaty to do so.

There may be other, and more indirect consequences of our accession to the Community on English legal thinking. These for the moment I ignore. Some judges, speaking with more zeal than discretion have already claimed that it is so, but, on the whole, where they have attempted to apply their doctrine, it has been shown that their argument is based on a degree of misunderstanding of what community law actually enjoins. One cannot rule out, of course, the long-term effects on judicial reasoning of familiarity with another tradition of jurisprudence. But, if the experience of the original six members is any guide, and by now it should be, these are likely to be more technical than require discussion here.

What does require discussion is the political consequence. Britain is part of a community of nine. Much of its commercial law, and many of its economic regulations require prolonged negotiation either with the Commission or in the Council of Ministers. Members of a new Community Parliament, not always, as heretofore, automatically members of the House of Commons or the House of Lords, will soon be coming on the scene, whatever the system of voting, representing vast areas far wider than our present constituencies, and the system of voting itself when, as it will be before long, it is made uniform throughout the Community, is not likely to be standardized on our present first past the post arrangements. Already it is clear that, if the Westminster Parliament is to retain anything like adequate control of ministers or economic policy, it will have to devote a great deal of Parliamentary time to the discussion of European matters, and, in a Parliament where Parliamentary time is as scarce as it is in the House of Commons, it is quite unlikely that this can be made available without a profound effect on our methods of legislation, and thus indirectly on our institutions themselves. If the case for less legislation, and a greater degree of devolution of legislative and administrative functions were not already compelling, it is clear that this new addition to the burden of Parliamentary membership would by itself make a powerful case for change.

It is also difficult to believe that the actual political divisions within Europe will leave our domestic party structures unaltered, certainly not in ethos, and possibly not in organization. Already Conservative members of the European Parliament are sitting, and acting in concert with, party groups from other countries like minded with themselves. It is at least probable that similar associations will be found by other British parties.

One immediate, though indirect, result of our European membership has been the introduction of the referendum into United Kingdom politics as a constitutional device. It was never possible that such an arrangement, once tried, should not be repeated. It has, at least in promise, been repeated already in the government's draft proposals for devolution. It seems hardly possible that matters will be left there. What is strange is that there has been practically no discussion as to how, or in what form, the institution should be systematized. Referenda are of different kinds. In what circumstances is it to be thought proper to have resort to one? It can hardly be left, as now, simply as a convenient escape route by which a divided Cabinet can avoid collective responsibility. Is the referendum to be taken before, or after legislation has passed Parliament? Is its effect to be conclusive or only advisory? If it is conclusive, is a simple majority enough, and, if so, must the majority apply to the whole, or to each of the principal parts of the United Kingdom? What subjects are to be referable? Who may set the machinery in motion? Is it to be the government, or Parliament, or may it, as in Switzerland, be called into being by a sizeable group of private citizens?

I do not claim to be able to answer these questions. The point I am making is that the consequences, immediate and indirect, of our membership of the Community, are certain to be such as to give impetus and urgency to any discussions now taking place on the future of our constitution, and to influence the result in favour of change and a closer definition of the powers and functions of Parliament. If for other reasons we are to face demands for a British Bill of Rights, for changed systems of voting, for a reformed second chamber, for devolution to regions, the impact of European membership can only be to make such discussions more urgent and the need for precise answers more definite. The unwritten and slowly evolving conventions which have served us so well and so long are hardly likely to survive unaltered when so much that is novel is forcing itself on our attention. The difficulty is to make our fellow countrymen take the discussion seriously in time to arrive at rational conclusions.

XXVIII

THE LOCAL
GOVERNMENT DIMENSION

A serious, and it may be a fatal, objection to much of what I have been writing is that, so far from providing new liberties, what I am suggesting is not less but more government, yet another turn of the screw, yet another tier or tiers to our already top-heavy constitutional edifice. At first sight there is force in this. We have already parishes, counties, boroughs, metropolitan districts, the Greater London Council, the Inner London Education Authority, Water Boards, Gas Boards, Electricity Boards, Hospital Areas and so on and so forth. We have Parliament, and, soon, we shall have a directly elected European Assembly as well as the Commission and Council of Ministers, and a whole bevy of other international organizations. Now, it may be urged, you are saddling us with a whole new tier, intermediate between the Counties, or Metropolitan Districts, and Westminster. It is too much. We are over-governed already, and you are giving us yet more.

I am myself quite clear in my own mind that the reorganization of local government which took place during Mr Heath's administration of which I was a member and which led to separate solutions in England (less London), Scotland, and Wales was controversial at the time it was passed and not by any means an unqualified success since it has been introduced. Moreover, the mere fact of any further change taking place so soon after structural reforms of as drastic a character is a difficult and unattractive concept. Better leave ill alone, if it means yet another upheaval. It may well be that this argument is irresistible.

I must, however, make some effort to defend myself. I would agree at once that the argument has a great deal of force as it applies to my proposals for devolved assemblies in the regions and in Scotland, Wales and Northern Ireland.

But it has no application at all to my proposals for a Bill of Rights, a proportionately elected second chamber, or a constitution limiting by law the right of Parliament to legislate without restriction. All these moves would be in the direction of less government and not more.

Secondly, even within the field where the objection has force, it is at least doubtful whether we shall be able to continue indefinitely without legislation. Some provision of some kind will sooner or later have to be made for Northern Ireland. It will not be possible indefinitely to go on there without either increasing the number of Members of Parliament or again devolving powers to a local elected assembly. If there is to be devolution in Scotland, I cannot for the life of me see how it can be avoided in Northern Ireland, and, although logically there seems no reason why, in the absence of regional government in England, Wales may not stay as it is, I have a feeling that Welsh public opinion might easily not allow this logical answer to be maintained. As I have said, I do not believe that Scotland will continue in the United Kingdom for ever without a devolved assembly, and, if I am right about all this, or any substantial part of it, the objection loses force, since we shall be driven to create the additional tier in some parts of the United Kingdom in any event, with all the problems that this will entail about the delimitation and policing of powers, methods of voting, finance and the relation between the local government reforms and the provincial assemblies.

Thirdly, I must protest that, whether or not I am advocating the impossible, the object of my proposals was not to create new governmental powers, but to hive off some of the existing powers so that what is now done in Whitehall, might be done more locally, and that what was done by ministers responsible to Westminster might be done by committees or local officers responsible to local assemblies. My object was that Parliament and its ministers should do less, not that some other bodies should perform new tasks not at present undertaken.

Lastly, if it is really true that the recent local government reforms are working as badly as I have heard it suggested, it may very well be that a revision of boundaries and functions, if found necessary, could better be done by locally elected assemblies than by Parliament operating through the large ministries in Whitehall and driving through the reformed arrangements by the guillotine on a pattern wholly uniform throughout the country.

There is, of course, something positive to be said in favour of regional or provincial governments. In the first place, the system of rates, which is the main source of local government taxation at present, is universally unpopular but has defied successive Royal Commissions and all political parties to find an effective alternative. It may well be that one reason at least for their failure has been the insufficiently large size of local units. Other countries, with larger units, have managed to solve the problem.

Secondly, there are in fact a number of functions requiring regional rather than local government treatment. At present these are not being dealt with adequately at all, or are being handled by new *ad hoc* boards, like the gas, water, and electricity authorities, or the new police authorities and the area hospital boards, or are being dealt with by central government in the form of regionalized centres of national government, of which the most conspicuous, though not by any means the only, examples are those in Edinburgh and Cardiff. If these could be brought together under a single general purpose authority, the result would be less government, not more.

I was particularly struck by this problem during the period of my responsibility for the North-East. So long as existing local authorities are made to deal with different functionalized government departments or services like education, roads, or housing, and functionalized boards like water, gas, electricity, and health, there can be no proper regionalized planning, and the existence of large nominated boards, most of which have developed since my time in the North-East, is really a move away from democratic control by general purpose elected bodies. It is, in the strictest sense, a reaction. Before the development of all-purpose local authorities at the end of the nineteenth century, boards like this were the fashion. They have developed again precisely because the units of local government, even as reconstituted, are too small to provide adequate geographical areas to plan, administer, or serve the communities for which they are designed. What is even more bewildering is the reversion to different geographical boundaries for different functions.

I am not at all convinced that a pattern of regional governments taking over many of the functions of central government and their regional offices, and many of the duties of functional area boards and joint police authorities would not pave the way in the end for a move towards an organization of local government on a much more decentralized basis than was thought possible at the time of the Heath reforms. It does not seem to me that it is necessary to form a concluded view on this. But whatever answer is given, two broad advantages would seem to me to result for central government with which I am personally more familiar.

In the first place life would be more tolerable for ministers and Members of Parliament. Nothing struck me more during my period of office as a minister than the extraordinary contrast between the relative leisure enjoyed by members of foreign legislative assemblies and their ministers, and our own. This has since been proved statistically. Members of Parliament put in something like five times as much time debating as do some of their European counterparts. I believe that this does nothing but harm both to the efficiency of individual members and of the legislative efficiency of Parliament itself. The burden on ministers is proportionately greater. Attendance at the House is virtually compulsory all the time. Ministers have to be sent for from the ends of the earth to attend important divisions. They have no time to visit their constituencies. They have no time to think. It is those who have leisure, as the author of the book Ecclesiasticus long ago pointed out, who become wise. If so we can hardly be surprised if our own ministers and Members of Parliament seem decreasingly endowed with this necessary characteristic.

My final point is that the new European dimension of government to which I drew attention in my last chapter will certainly not diminish the burden on ministers and members of the Westminster Parliament, even if we abandon, as I suppose we shall, the compulsory dual membership which imposes such an intolerable additional burden on individuals. Parliament will have more and more constantly to discuss the impact of Community rules and regulations on domestic policy. The relationship of these and other international conventions to national and regional policy is not something which can be passed by in silence and debates in Westminster, particularly in the House of Lords, are being mounted with increasing frequency. If in fact Parliament is to do its work properly it simply must slough off some of its existing work. The existing structure of local government in England, Northern Ireland, Scotland and Wales does not permit this. It is perhaps time that we created a model capable of bearing the load.

XXIX

VOTING SYSTEMS

There is a powerful case for some sort of electoral reform. I wish, however, to dispose of or at least criticize some of the arguments which, though plausible, I do not regard as convincing, and, before making some positive suggestions I wish to explain some countervailing considerations of which I believe account should be taken.

Ever since I can remember electoral reform has been passionately advocated by the Liberal Party. As presented by them, the argument is usually put as follows. Take the voting at the last election, whenever the last election happens to have been at the time, or the last few elections. Count the votes cast for the various parties throughout the country. Divide these totals by the number of seats in the House of Commons. Compare them with the actual seats which have in fact been gained by the various parties, and you see immediately a considerable disparity in favour of the large parties and against the Liberals and though doubtfully and occasionally, against other parties. The conclusion you draw is that the Liberals are under-represented and should have been allotted a sizeable number of seats in proportion to their total vote in the country.

Given certain assumptions, there is obviously considerable force in this. But, before it is accepted hook, line and sinker, there are some criticisms which must be made. The first is that the parties, as they exist today, including the Liberals, are themselves, to a large extent, the product of the voting system, and not static groupings with an inherent right to separate representation whenever there is a general election. There are approximately thirteen or fourteen different systems of voting current throughout the world. Each one of these, if applied in Britain over a period of years, would produce party groups different from the present. There is no *a priori* reason to suppose that, after ten years of a different system, any of the existing parties would exist at all in their present form. They are all groupings designed to produce results under the existing system.

As a matter of fact I happen to believe that some systems of electoral reform would greatly benefit the Labour Party, so long, that is, as they continued to maintain their organic relationship with the Trade Union movement. I believe this is not the view commonly held in Transport House or the Conservative Central Office, and it is, of course, highly speculative. But it is at least consistent with the experience of the Scandinavian countries where the equivalents of the Labour Party have remained in power with an absolute majority for periods up to forty years, and the equivalents of the Liberal and Conservative Parties have broken down into a number of separate party groups, none exactly coincident with British Liberal or Conservative Party organization and almost permanently in opposition. Since I do not believe that permanent single-party government is either beneficial to the national interest or compatible with real democracy, I find this possibility unattractive.

The second criticism I make is that the disparity between votes and seats is not entirely the consequence of the present first past the post voting system. It is in part due to the unequal distribution of party support geographically. This can be seen conveniently by looking at any electoral map. To cite an extreme case, to the extent that party votes are concentrated in safe seats, most of these are bound to be 'wasted'. If some could be transferred to marginal seats, quite a different result would be obtained. But this result would not necessarily be more representative, or more democratic. A large country like ours must have Members of Parliament who do in fact represent local communities. So far as regards Scotland, which, partly in consequence of population changes, is grossly over-represented on a numerical basis, this has been recognized since the Act of Union. In a large country, population numbers cannot be the sole criterion for separate representation.

Another, and equally potent, factor in the present unequal representation is the universality of the single-member constituency, itself of fairly recent origin. But this too has advantages which many would prefer to the various alternatives. Multi-member constituencies do not, on the whole, work very well, and it is doubtful whether a change over to them would be popular. If there were a referendum in which it was clearly explained to the voters that one result of any move towards electoral reform in any of the ways likely to be adopted in place of the present system would be the loss of 'their' Member of Parliament, and 'their' representation instead by a multi-member team covering a much wider area, it is by no means certain that the case for reform would win.

My conclusion is that, although, at the end of the day, there is an irreducible amount of weight to be allowed to the classical Liberal case, it is not convincingly made out in the form in which it is generally propounded.

One of the advantages claimed for a change in system is that it would benefit moderation in politics. This has not been borne out either in Northern Ireland or in parts of Europe. The truth is that, where there is a polarization between two or three communities, or two or three political extremes, reformed systems of voting tend to give less power to moderates in the control of their own extremists, and more bargaining power to extremists in their negotiation with the moderate wing of their own way of thinking, and in the wheeling and dealing between leaders after the result of the election is known. This can be extremely serious. The political stability which has resulted from the control by the left-wing and centre of the Conservative Party of fringe movements of the right, and, until the advent of Mr Wilson, the control by the right and centre of the Labour Party of the Communists or fringe movements of the left, has been of great national benefit. It should not lightly be cast away.

To translate this into Northern Irish terms, you do not in fact see moderate members of the SDLP exchanging second preference votes with, or even adopting conciliatory attitudes towards, moderate Unionists, or vice versa. What has been seen is the spectacle of the moderates of both sides coming under continuous threats or pressure from the extremists on their own side and so rendering 'power sharing' or even normal majority rule impossible. To translate into European terms, the large Communist parties in France and Italy, the communal parties in Belgium, and the rise of the Nazis in the Weimar Republic after they had obtained a foothold in the Reichstag, are not very effective advertisements for any system of electoral reform. The success of a slightly more sophisticated system in Bonn and, of the civilized, if largely one-party dominated, process of government in the Scandinavian countries is not a conclusive countervailing argument. At most it can be said that, given a moderate and mature electorate and an absence of external danger, electoral reform need not necessarily be fatal to democracy. Changes in the voting system would almost certainly benefit the Communists, who advocate a system of proportional representation, and the National Front. Any possible advantage to the Liberals is far more doubtful.

There is a further disadvantage in reformed systems of voting which I do not believe has been given adequate weight. The real object of any electoral system must be to create a structure of government which reflects the genuine wishes of the people, so far as these can be reliably ascertained. That is indeed, the principal advantage claimed for reformed systems. But it is arguable that they do not in fact achieve this result. So far as the result may be to produce a large number of party groupings, none of which can reasonably hope to form a government, the genuine wishes of the people, at least arguably, are not reflected in the result actually obtained. The controlling factor in determining the government actually formed is not the vote of the electors, but the terms of the bargain, or, perhaps more significantly, the succession of bargains, struck during the fixed term of a Parliament by the different party groups within it. This does not make for consistency of policy or the control by the electors of what actually happens. It is more likely to lead to unprincipled compromises than stable and effective government reflecting the popular will.

What then is the true case for electoral reform, and where does it lead us? Personally, I can see nothing intrinsically objectionable in the largest organized minority forming the executive government with all that that entails in the way of control of administrative and financial policy, provided that this right does not carry with it an unlimited licence to legislate. It is not self-evident that executive government and the right to legislate should be in the same hands or subject to identical limitations. The American constitution effectively and of set intention precludes this from happening. The executive government is in the hands of a President elected on a nation-wide constituency by what is virtually a close approximation to our own first past the post system. The legislature, subject to the limitations enforced by the Supreme Court, contains two Houses elected by differently organized constituencies. The present constitution of France is designed to achieve a not dissimilar effect, and, in different parts of the world, other variants exist. I always suspect those who say that the Westminster model is not sacrosanct, but in this context I am bound to say so myself.

Can general principles be teased out of these complex and conflicting arguments? For myself, I think they can. I believe the executive government should govern according to the principles on which it is elected. I can see no objection in principle to a system of voting which enables a single party to form an administration on these lines. What is intolerable is that such a government should treat a slender majority in the House of Commons obtained by this means as a licence to carry through irreversible changes against the desires of a majority of the electorate on the pretext that these proposals, or some of them, were contained in the election manifesto. This is just what has been happening in recent years, and those of us who value our ancient liberties must make sure that it never happens again. The very fact that the main advocates of our present arrangement are the leaders of the Labour left fills me with alarm, and the circumstance that the same figures advocate the abolition, without replacement, of the House of Lords, and attack the judiciary every time a court decision is handed down which offends their political associates, does nothing to diminish my anxiety. I would certainly prefer almost any system of electoral reform to the prospect of elective dictatorship in any form, but particularly one based on first past the post voting.

For consider what it really would mean. It is amply established that our present system of voting can install in office a government representing no more than a minority of those who voted, and perhaps no more than a quarter of the total electorate, and that the whips and the guillotine combined can drive through the House of Commons almost any legislation acceptable to the majority virtually without discussion, and without the minimum delay necessary to give public opinion a chance to make its weight felt. It is also clearly established since the war that the prerogative of dissolution in the hands of a skilful Prime Minister can manipulate the timing of an election to give a better than even chance on the present system of voting of perpetuating his rule. To give a single chamber elected by this means unlimited powers, not even trammelled with the vestigial rights of delay now remaining in the hands of the present House of Lords, would be in fact to establish an elective dictatorship, based on minority rule, since the House of Commons, elected by this manner, would have neither legal nor political limits imposed upon it, and, in theory at least, could even prolong its own life. It is clear that, against such a regime, electoral reform, whatever its disadvantages, would be a preferable alternative, and, if the only acceptable alternative, an absolutely essential change for any believer in liberty under law.

But is it the only acceptable alternative? Personally I see no reason at all why the same system of voting should be established for local government, Parliament, the European Parliament, and, if we have them, regional assemblies, or a reformed House of Lords. If, as I propose, we should have an elected second chamber, and regional assemblies, there would be nothing to prevent the regional assemblies being elected on one system, if it were thought appropriate, the House of Commons on a second, the European Parliament on whatever system is agreed between the nine (or twelve) after 1978, and the elective second chamber on a fourth. Obviously so many different systems are intrinsically undesirable. But two or three, namely the present, first past the post, party lists, and STV, would be perfectly workable, and, if one system proved to be more acceptable than the others in practice it could be standardized throughout. Personally, I would prefer the present system for the House of Commons, STV for the regional assemblies, and either

STV or party lists for the House of Lords and Europe. What is not tolerable is that the present method should continue without a more effective control on the majority in the House of Commons than is provided by the present House of Lords or without some limitations on the kind of legislation that can pass through Parliament without directly consulting the people.

THE POWER
OF DISSOLUTION

The legal powers of Parliament are unlimited. It can even prolong its own life, as, with general approval, did the Parliament of 1935 during the Second, and the Parliament of 1910 during the First World War. At a time when a general election, even if not actually impossible, would have been a great inconvenience and probably have produced a wholly unrepresentative result, this was undoubtedly a great boon.

In time of peace, this possible use of power presents a threat to liberty more theoretical than real, though I would not place it beyond the capacity of an extreme government of the right or the left to misuse it in conditions of economic crisis. The framers of the Parliament Act 1911 were evidently of the same opinion, since they made the prolongation of the life of a Parliament conditional on the consent of both Houses. They may not, however, have succeeded in achieving their object in this singularly ill-drafted piece of legislation, since the Act does not expressly preclude the abolition of the House of Lords under the Parliament Act procedure, and since, under the Act of 1949, the Lords' power of delay is reduced effectively to one year, it would then be open to a sufficiently unscrupulous government to abolish the House of Lords in the first two sessions of a Parliament and prolong its own life thereafter by the vote of the Commons, guillotined if necessary, in the third, unless the courts read the Parliament Acts in such a way as to leave the abolition of the House of Lords as a matter still requiring the consent of both Houses. Although no one would pretend that this is an acute or immediately serious danger, it is sufficiently important as a matter of theoretical possibility to make it desirable to deal with it in one way or another.

Far more actual is the danger inherent in the unlimited

prerogative of the Crown to grant a dissolution, at any point of time during the life of a Parliament. Ever since the early days of the Third Republic this has always been recognized by French Republicans as a possible instrument of dictatorship, and it is worth considering whether it is not developing on these lines here. Under our law, the maximum time that a Parliament may sit (unless prolonged by Act of Parliament) is five years, having been reduced from a previous seven at which Walpole had fixed it in the early eighteenth century precisely in order to avoid defeat at a general election.

Undoubtedly, since 1945, successive governments have found the prerogative of dissolution extremely useful. In practice, during these years, the sovereign has granted a dissolution at any time at which the reigning Prime Minister has so advised, and the effect of this can be seen by the use to which reigning Prime Ministers have in fact put the prerogative. Since 1945, there have been general elections in 1950, 1951, 1955, 1959, 1964, 1966, 1970 and 1974 (two elections). In these elections the opposition has succeeded in securing a change only in 1951, 1964, 1970 and 1974 (the first election). In each of these the government of the day has only been beaten by the narrowest of margins, notwithstanding that, according to opinion polls and by-elections alike, the climate of public opinion has been almost consistently hostile to the government in office.

To treat this as coincidental would, at least in my view, be extremely naïve. One may criticize the opinion polls as much as one likes, and I am the last person to suggest that by themselves they are not often misleading. But I can only say that in giving advice to the Prime Minister between 1957 and 1959 as to when it would be in the interest of the party to secure a dissolution, I watched the opinion polls, together with by-elections, and local elections and other signs of the political weather, like a lynx. Moreover, although it was nothing to do with me in my capacity as party chairman, I could not fail to know that, with the power possessed by any government to influence the economy, it would be asking too much of any Prime Minister not to attempt, by any means in his power, to create a period of relatively fine economic weather to coincide with his going to the polls. Indeed it is arguably his duty to do so. To hold an election in a period of economic instability would be to encourage speculation of the worst possible kind and lead to currency fluctuations which would certainly not be in the interests of the nation.

However this may be, it would be simple minded not to recognize that the prerogative of dissolution makes changes of government much more difficult to achieve, and, though it may be desirable to retain it either unaltered or in some modified form, it would be wrong not to include it in our calculations in considering the importance or value of other constitutional changes required to diminish the danger of our developing into an elective dictatorship controlled by a highly organized minority of electors.

Against such a danger, the undoubted remaining power of the Queen is no effective safeguard. Could the Crown refuse a dissolution demanded by an unscrupulous Prime Minister or dismiss a Prime Minister who refused to ask for one? Possibly it could in extreme circumstances, since, as I have tried to show, the Crown is the ultimate guarantor of constitutional government against takeover by an authoritarian regime. But that it would certainly be a desperate remedy is clearly shown by the experience in Australia of Sir John Kerr and the experience of the late Lord Byng in Canada in 1921. In each case, the monarchy became a subject of controversy, in spite of the fact that in each case the refusal of the prerogative was not a decision of the actual sovereign, but of an appointee of the Crown made on the advice of responsible ministers, in Sir John Kerr's case of the same Prime Minister who was complaining of his own dismissal. If the decision was that of the sovereign himself a crisis of this kind would be far more serious and might even put the continued existence of the monarchy in question. Admittedly, as I pointed out in an earlier chapter, there is a fail-safe mechanism.

Nonetheless, it must be said that, once a major national party put the abolition of the monarchy on its list of political agenda, it would only be a matter of time before the monarchy was abolished unless in the interval that party itself lost its political life or dropped the republican item from its programme. The monarchy can survive only so long as the parties who possess a real chance of winning continue to support it. When this ceases to be the case, the pendulum will ultimately swing to the party supporting a republican programme. The monarch, therefore, who ventured to use the prerogative against either of the two major parties of the state would risk either enforced abdication or republicanism, and even if the action of the Crown was confirmed by the electorate, there would be uncertainty and controversy for a long time thereafter. The conclusion is that the monarchy itself is not an adequate safeguard against misuse of the prerogative of dissolution, except in extreme and desperate conditions calling in question the whole constitution of the state.

Does the solution lie in Parliaments with a fixed term, or in which a proportion of the members retire every year as in the American Senate, or as happens with certain local authorities here? Obviously there is something to be said in favour of such a policy. Other nations manage to survive, retain their freedom, and preserve continuity and relative efficiency by these methods. It is, therefore, impossible to argue *a priori* that such an arrangement could not succeed in Britain.

But there are disadvantages, and these should not be underestimated. A country does not necessarily thrive best if it suffers from prolonged, or worse still, continuous bouts of election fever. In all fixed-term constitutions, as election time approaches, it becomes much more difficult to get anything positive done, and the period immediately after an election can be almost worse, since parties have adopted stances during the campaign from which it is difficult to resile, and which are concerned more with vote-getting than either justice or efficiency.

My own belief is that our own system is the best, but only provided that greater control can be exercised over the majority in the House of Commons, by some or preferably all of the possible remedies. It has been suggested to me that a further safeguard would be provided if my proposed elective second chamber were elected by rotational retirement or for fixed terms, so that elections to it did not coincide with those to the Commons.

I admit the theoretical point, but would counter it by the following practical considerations.

In the first place I do not wish the second chamber to be a court of appeal against the real verdict of the electors. To my way of thinking, the essence of democracy is a statement about sovereignty residing in the electorate, and sovereignty includes the power and right to make mistakes. The object of what I am proposing is not in any way to limit the sovereignty of the people but to keep the House of Commons from developing its tendency to become an elective dictatorship. If, at a general election, the electorate chooses to return not merely a government representing the highest organized minority, but a Parliament in which there is an absolute majority in both Houses for radical legislation, though I might continue to oppose that legislation in debate, I would not wish to render it more difficult to pass than the weight of argument or human rights entrenched in the constitution could make it.

In the second place, I do not wish to see an elective second chamber becoming the dominant partner. This would defeat one of my chief objects. This is to have a strong government, where possible in the hands of a single party with a mandate to govern, even where the proportional support in the electorate is not sufficient to give it the right to put its entire legislative programme into effect. I visualize my second chamber as occupying a subordinate role, whose function is to control the legislative powers of Parliament in the interests of the electorate as a whole, without undue interference with the executive powers of government. I do not visualize it either as reflecting some previous balance between the parties at an earlier election, or as representing a balance of public opinion more up to date than that represented in the House of Commons. If that happened, until the House of Commons altered its own method of election, the power of the second chamber would be equal to, or greater than, that of the Commons, and this would both stultify the process of government and lead to prolonged controversy. I would thus leave the power of dissolution where it is, in the hands of a Prime Minister dependent for his continued existence upon the support of the Commons alone. If, for any reason, he felt that the action of the elective second chamber was unduly restrictive, irresponsible, or otherwise out of touch with public opinion, he would be free to test the matter by an appeal to the sovereign electorate.

XXXI

COALITIONS AND NATIONAL GOVERNMENTS

The main thrust of my argument so far has been to favour constitutional change. But I am sure that at some stage someone may wish to argue that there is an alternative. If our constitution is breaking down, it will be said that this is because of the vehemence of party feeling. Why not form a coalition government of all parties, or a national government consisting of all the best elements in the nation? So, it is often said, we could form an administration which could manage the trade unions, but which could be trusted not to go in for any specifically socialist measures like nationalization. There have been few occasions during the past twenty years when I have not been assailed by arguments of this kind, usually from people with whose views I ordinarily agree and for whose characters I entertain respect. In the past couple of years this approach has had distinguished adherents in Mr Harold Macmillan and Lord Duncan Sandys.

It is not, perhaps, surprising that patriotically minded people should turn their thoughts in this direction, inspired, no doubt, by memories of wartime co-operation, and possibly by memories of the events of 1931.

Before enquiring whether such an arrangement is desirable it is worth discussing what exactly it is designed to achieve and in what conditions it would be possible to set it up.

There are some people who frankly wish to set up a coalition because they believe that the medicine the country needs to swallow is so unpleasant and so urgently necessary that there is no prospect of administering the dose successfully under the full rigour and rancour of party warfare. There may be something in this, even though it might be thought doubtfully democratic, but it is certainly not compatible with the other great argument used in favour of coalition, which is that the see-saw effect which, it is said, has been the characteristic of recent governments of opposite political complexion would thereby be avoided. This argument would tend to achieve compromise rather than the administration of unpleasant medicine, but I do not myself believe that there is anything in it. In so far as there has been a see-saw effect, it has, I believe, been due to the determination on the left of the Labour Party to produce irreversible changes in a socialist direction. The see-saw consists in the oscillation set up by measures of this kind introduced by Labour Governments and attempts by their Conservative successors to reverse them. If any particular policies of either party are considered to be too extreme to be desirable in the interests of national unity, the remedy lies in constitutional changes designed to prevent irreversible changes or extreme measures unless and until these are really supported by a majority of the electorate.

Advocates of coalitions often point to the relative stability of composite governments abroad, particularly on the continent of Europe. But normally these are operating in conditions of Parliaments elected for a fixed term. The members are locked in together for a fixed period of time. During this time there is an obligation to make things work, sometimes better, and sometimes worse. In Britain the power of dissolution offers a means of escape.

The fact of the matter is that coalitions are the product of a parliamentary situation, and, in the absence of appropriate conditions, are not so much undesirable as impossible. So long as the Prime Minister and the Cabinet can command a majority in the House of Commons, a coalition cannot happen in time of peace without the consent of the governing party. If the majority is lost, the Prime Minister has the option of asking for a dissolution or trying to form a new composite Cabinet. He can only succeed if such an arrangement can command a stable majority. If, during the course of a Parliament, a composite government is formed and then wishes to appeal to the country it can only do so if some kind of *ad hoc* arrangement is made in the constituencies, as happened in the 'coupon' election of 1918, and in the election called in 1931. In the absence of conditions which make a coalition government possible it makes no sense at all to call for the creation of one. In 1974 an attempt, which I favoured, was made to create a Liberal and Conservative coalition, but this was after the February election and designed to meet the parliamentary situation created by the result. In the event it failed since the Liberals did not accept our proposals. If they had agreed, the success or failure of the coalition would have depended on its ability to formulate a policy which commanded a majority in the House of Commons of that time. My own belief is that, though the attempt was worth while, it would probably have failed to get a majority for the Queen's Speech.

Wartime coalitions are formed for rather different reasons, but are still the product of the parliamentary situation of the time. While criticism in time of war may be valuable, and while Parliament still has a valuable part to play, organized opposition on party lines is impossible, and a general election at least difficult. The object of a wartime coalition is to prevent organized opposition in Parliament on condition that the majority party does not abuse its position, and this can only be achieved by a substantial agreement between the parties under the terms of which neither party is entitled to pursue its internal aims in Parliament whilst hostilities continue.

I feel I must here draw a distinction between a coalition and a national government. In modern Parliamentary language a coalition is when two parties agree that their leaders should work together in a single Cabinet. The government is then composed of the leaders of both parties and the government majority is that formed by the combined votes of their rank and file. Churchill's Government during the war was such a coalition, but its elements flew apart after the end of hostilities with Germany and before the end of the war with Japan. Lloyd George's Coalition succeeded in maintaining its existence after the armistice in 1918, but likewise flew apart so soon as the Conservatives decided to withdraw their support after the Carlton Club meeting. Ramsay MacDonald's first National Government remained a true coalition only so long as the Samuelite Liberals, supported by their members in the Commons, remained in the Cabinet. When they withdrew, because of their continued adherence to the principle of Free Trade, after the Ottawa agreements, the National Government continued, but ceased to be a coalition in any real sense, since it was kept in being by the vast Conservative majority and did not depend for its continued existence on the support of the back benchers of any other party.

There is something to be said for a national government of this kind supported by a single-party majority but whose ministers represent a wider spectrum of opinion. It is, perhaps, begging a number of questions to describe such an administration as truly national. All the same it has merits over and above its party support. The presence in its ranks of members who are not members of the ruling party gives a fairly adequate guarantee that its measures will not be deliberately or violently partisan. It has also the merit of relative durability. In British parliamentary conditions, the weakness of coalitions is their inherent instability. The gap which inevitably separates front and back benchers is inexorably widened. The two groups of back benchers tend to treat such compromise as a betrayal while each separate section of the government is looking backwards over its shoulders at its own band of supporters, each situated in a different corner of the House, and equally suspicious that its leaders in the administration are surrendering principle to uneasy compromise. The condemnation which party zealots pronounced so eagerly on Butskellism in the 1950s becomes far more vigorous when two parties with divergent principles combine to form a single Cabinet, their leaders necessarily bound to preserve the confidence of their colleagues and defend their mistakes, the followers suspiciously eyeing every move, and threatening ever and anon to withdraw their sanction from the arrangement. When, however, a government is formed with a solid enough majority of the leader's own party, but is able to count on a spectrum of support in the country wider than that afforded by the party faithful, considerable advantage can be reaped, and there is not the same danger of an early split.

Mr Macmillan was always asserting that the last purely Conservative administration which he had heard of was that of Disraeli in 1874. There is some truth in this. The great paradox of the Conservative Party has been its capacity to survive, while all the Conservative parties on the continent of

Europe disappeared into smoke and mist or became disregarded and unimportant rumps representing only the most backward areas of the countryside. There have been prophets who have predicted the same dismal fate for British Conservatives. So far they have proved wrong, and this is due to the successive transfusions of blood which the British party has received from time to time from moderate opinion without positive affiliations, or from dissidents from their political adversaries, who have broken away from their own party because they disagreed with it on some fundamental point of policy. So the Liberal Unionists continued to fertilize the Conservative benches from the later 1880s until after the First World War, and when their influence had ceased to be distinguishable from the main stream of Conservatism as the result of the events of 1922, a new influx arrived in the wake of the Gold Standard crisis of 1931. Successive Conservative Governments in the thirties included or were supported by eminent persons previously of Liberal or Labour persuasion who, for one reason or another, found themselves disgusted by the economic policies propounded in the name of the Labour Party. Until comparatively recently there were constituencies in which supporters of the Conservative Party found it not merely advantageous, but truly informative, to describe themselves by some qualifying adjective such as National Liberals, and to have a separate political organization both in the field and in the House of Commons. I do not myself believe that Conservative Governments were the poorer for their presence, nor that their influence failed to influence the Conservative leadership in the direction of common sense and moderation.

My personal belief is that party government only leads to national prosperity in this country if the Conservative Party is led from left of its own centre and the Labour Party, or whatever may be the radical party of the day, is led from their right. This was largely the case until the advent of Mr Wilson and a great deal that has gone wrong since is due to the fact that though he is not himself a man of extreme views, he tried to lead the Labour Party from its left.

There would be no excuse if the Conservative Party were to fall into an analogous error. I am, of course, aware that in

Conservative terms, the expressions left and right are misleading. Left-wing Conservatives can be categorized according as to whether their radical characteristics are more liberal or more socialist. Mr Macmillan was an example of the left-wing Conservative of the socialist type. Baldwin was a left-wing Conservative liberal. But both favoured the pragmatic approach to politics and this, after all, is one of the most valuable assets the Conservative Party has brought to bear on national life. There is room in Conservatism for high Tory traditionalists, just as there is room in the Labour Party for some near Marxists. But I would begin to despair of our future in proportion as in either party the extremists were seen to gain the upper hand. It was with a genuine sense of relief that I saw Mr Callaghan succeed to the Labour Party leadership. I hope he succeeds in retaining it, even if, as I also hope, the Labour Party has a long period of opposition ahead.

There is another type of arrangement, distinct from coalition or national government, which can keep a party in office without permitting it to have its legislative freedom. This is the situation in which a third party supports a party government that could not survive without its help. This situation occurred in 1910 when the Irish Nationalists gave their support to the Liberal Party of the day in return for a pledge of Home Rule. It also occurred in 1923 and 1929 when the Liberal Party supported the two minority Labour Governments. It was suggested, but unsuccessfully, as a means of breaking the party deadlock after the first election of 1974. As I write, an arrangement of the same kind is operating between Mr Steel and Mr Callaghan.

The characteristic of such a situation is that the larger of the two parties carries the full responsibility for government, and the smaller carries with it the ability to bring the government down at any moment of its choosing. Whatever else can be said of such a situation the omens are unpropitious for the participants. In the aftermath, the Irish Nationalists were destroyed by Sinn Fein, as I believe to the infinite disadvantage of Ireland and the British Isles. The Liberals split into two hostile factions during the First World War and never satisfactorily came together again. In both the Labour minority governments the experience proved equally unsatisfactory for the Labour and the Liberal Parties. What will come of the present arrangement will be seen, but it does not seem impossible that history will repeat itself.

The purpose of this chapter is to make a simple point. None of the parliamentary devices which I have sought to describe is a substitute for constitutional reform. What we have to secure is not an alliance between incompatibles but that a reasonable distinction is drawn between the responsibilities of government which can legitimately be given to the party commanding the largest organized minority, and an unlimited licence to legislate in a partisan sense. The first can be given to the largest organized minority, the latter should be available only to a party or a combination of parties representing the real wishes of the nation. Devices, such as coalition, are no excuse for retaining the unlimited right to legislate, and are a poor substitute for a government which knows its own mind and is supported by a majority in the House of Commons. The possibilities of achieving good by such a device are extremely remote, and to use it as an alternative to constitutional reform would merely ensure that the danger of elective dictatorship would return before many years had elapsed or many Parliaments had been elected.

XXXII

PRIME MINISTER
AND CABINET

My argument so far has sought to establish two general points. Our unwritten constitution is breaking down. This cannot be remedied by any *ad hoc* tinkering with this element rather than that. The working parts of the rather complex machine which we have inherited are closely balanced and interference with one would inevitably affect the working of the others. Of all the working parts which I have examined so far only the Crown seems to be operating more or less satisfactorily as it is designed to do. The Commons is breaking down from overwork and a rush of self-importance to the head. The two-party system has produced what may be described either as an undesirable see-saw movement or as a vicious circle of events in which overspending is followed by economic crisis, economic crisis by inflation, inflation by panic measures designed to restore confidence, panic measures by reduced economic growth and unemployment, and unemployment to renewed overspending. As the result of the undemocratic nature of its composition, the House of Lords is unable to use even its inadequate powers so as to perform the necessary functions of a second chamber. The Civil Service, through no fault of its own, operates to strengthen the power of the executive and, at the receiving end of government, appears overblown, remote, and oppressive. The machine in Whitehall and Westminster fails to command the loyalty of minorities, and this in turn operates to create overtly separatist movements, pressure groups, or campaigns for legal restrictions on the powers of Parliament. The voting system allows even relatively small minorities of electors to dominate the majority. The organic connection between the unions and the Labour Party can be used to sabotage the policies of Conservative Governments, and, during Labour Governments to alienate the middle class and all those whose interests are not directly being pressed by trade union muscle. The volume of legislation, particularly of politically contentious legislation, prevents adequate discussion. While they can strike down the actions of ministers, the courts are impotent in the face of statute. The whole presents the picture of the City of Destruction, a national society in decline, whose institutions are no longer serving the needs of society and which, on my reading of history, is therefore likely, if left unaltered, to move slowly into anarchy or tyranny, and, more probably, the one followed by the other. I have tried to dispose of the notion that this combination of evils can be reversed by any simple, or single, device, and, in particular, by any device which does not involve a radical redesign of the whole machine, and therefore of all the constituent parts.

The one institution I have not so far separately examined is the Cabinet, and this necessarily involves the position of the Prime Minister who sits at the centre of the table and chairs its proceedings.

I have never been one of those who believe that the development of the office of Prime Minister has been in the direction of presidential government on the French or American models. In theory, this cannot be the case as long as we retain the hereditary monarchy as the one source of legitimate authority. In practice too, it cannot be the case because, in Whitehall, the Prime Minister does not command an office capable of dominating the vast feudal armies now controlled by the separate ministries and kept in a state of uneasy tension with one another by the network of ministerial and official committees which make government decisions and give effect to the government policy embodied in them. Unlike those of his senior colleagues and despite the sophisticated system of security and communications network, the Prime Minister's own office in Downing Street is no more than an enlarged private office.

The Cabinet Office from which alone central direction proceeds is not the Prime Minister's office, any more in fact than in name. In practice, no minister really inspects or controls its machinery. The Prime Minister's authority derives from his capacity to control the selection and enforce resignation of ministers, his power to create and control the personnel attending both the standing Cabinet committees and the secret *ad hoc* committees or informal groups of ministers, and his ultimate power to advise a dissolution in the event of government proving difficult or impossible. It is a system which encourages deviousness in Prime Ministers, and it has certainly been served by Prime Ministers who have acquired a reputation for deviousness.

But in truth, as well as in theory, the source of authority remains the Cabinet. Any senior minister who is unhappy at the direction taken by government decisions, or who has serious disagreements with his colleagues can bring his troubles to the Cabinet room, and, though, of course, a Prime Minister in the Chair can exercise an immense influence on the outcome by the various arts, white and black, of skilful chairmanship, he cannot effectively stake his own will against the determined opposition of colleagues. This is because, unlike the members of the Cabinet of the United States, who are simply the President's creatures, the members of the British Cabinet are also Members of Parliament. If the Prime Minister forced their resignation they would pursue their opposition to his policies on the floor of one House or the other, and from that platform they are irremoveable until after a general election and then only by the electorate. I know of no recent case where the Prime Minister of the day has advised the Crown to dissolve Parliament simply as the result of a disagreement on policy with his colleagues.

The Cabinet, therefore, has an effective veto on decisions. But a divided Cabinet is not a particularly apt body to take contentious decisions. For one thing, it is much too large, and, for another, the number of decisions to be taken is far too numerous to be discussed at all, still less to be thrashed out in a full sitting. Although the Cabinet has not gone the way of the Privy Council and become a formal piece of government machinery designed to register and give legal effect to decisions in fact arrived at elsewhere, on many matters of importance it is well on the way to getting there. Recent Cabinet memoirs have rightly insisted that the Cabinet minutes give no inkling of the real course of discussions. This is not to agree with the late Richard Crossman that they are concocted. They are no more concocted than the Journals of the House of Commons or the House of Lords which, unlike Hansard, but like Cabinet minutes, make no attempt to record individual utterances. Like the Journals, Cabinet minutes are essential records of decisions taken with just sufficient additional information to enable the Civil Service, which has to act on them, to understand the policy. They are no substitute for private records like the Crossman diaries. But they are not intended to be.

The fact, however, is that, on matters of importance, the Cabinet as such is usually consulted fairly late in the day. The ground has already been carefully prepared by discussions between civil servants, correspondence between ministers, informal meetings, Cabinet committee meetings, whether of standing Cabinet committees, like those on economic policy or on foreign affairs and defence, or of special, and not always static, groups of ministers or *ad hoc* committees. By the time the Cabinet is brought in as a whole, it may very well be that only one decision is possible, even when, had it been consulted at the outset, the policy would have been wholly unacceptable.

Though the Cabinet remains, therefore, at the seat of power, the idea that it still sits as the real fountain of policy, like the Cabinets of Disraeli, Gladstone, or Asquith, is misleading. Many ministers of considerable standing and influence are not in the Cabinet at all. The government itself is something more than a hundred strong, and one, at least contributory, factor in the power of modern governments to control the House of Commons resides in the fact that the members of the government, who include the natural leaders of almost every faction in the majority party, by themselves form one of the largest groups in the whole House, keep potential revolts without effective leadership and can deliver, at the crack of the whip, with their Parliamentary private secretaries, about one hundred and twenty-five automatic votes in a division to support contentious policies.

But the Cabinet itself has ceased to be the monolithic body which, in theory, it remains, and, in practice, once was. On three separate occasions during my adult life the formal unity of the Cabinet has been openly breached. The first was the 'agreement to differ' proposed by my father during his frantic, and in the end unsuccessful, endeavour to keep the Liberals in the government at the time of Ottawa. The second was the device adopted by Mr Wilson's Government during the referendum campaign about Britain's continued membership of the European Community. The third is the licence to differ given by Mr Callaghan by which his colleagues may disagree on direct elections to the European Parliament. Thus the government of Britain is no longer in practice what it is in theory.

Quite apart from these occasional breaches of Cabinet responsibility, the loyalties which used to hold colleagues together are breaking down. As recently as in Mr Macmillan's Cabinet it would have been unthinkable for ministers to keep diaries like Richard Crossman's, let alone to publish them, or allow them to be published posthumously. I can remember that there was quite a painful scene on one occasion when one member was observed to be taking notes of what was being said, so far as I know for the perfectly proper purpose of replying to a discussion in which he was interested. But the tendency has been for a whole rash of memoirs, all more or less indiscreet, to follow the end of governments, and the publication of Richard Crossman's diaries, sanctioned, alas, by a decision of the Lord Chief Justice, was only the latest and most blatant, and not the only example, of its type.

The advent of political advisers and special public relations officers is another example of the crumbling of the old view of Cabinet responsibility. These politically motivated assistants habitually disclose to the press information about the views of individual ministers for the precise purpose of mobilizing public opinion against colleagues who take an opposite point of view, even when the leak does not come from ministers themselves in contact with lobby correspondents and individual editors. My own view for what it is worth is that the old-style doctrine of Cabinet responsibility can only survive at all so long as Cabinets are composed of members of a single party. If ever Cabinets became formal coalitions, the need to keep junior ministers and influential back benchers in touch would, when added to the pressures already operating, completely disintegrate the remaining ramparts of Cabinet secrecy and responsibility. The Cabinet would become like any other committee of which the membership is mixed and responsible to different caucuses.

There are a number of sources of misunderstanding which, I believe, would astonish even a well-informed person who attended a series of meetings of a real Cabinet. Certainly they used to surprise me. The first would be the inordinate amount of time spent on discussing the details of government business in the House of Commons during the current week. The newcomer might be equally surprised at the long and rambling discussions of the day-to-day issues in foreign affairs. These are usually raised orally at the beginning of the meeting whereas matters requiring long-term consideration in domestic policy, when discussed at all, are normally focused by a paper circulated in advance, and placed relatively low on the agenda, so that they are frequently given insufficient consideration. Thirdly, if he ever attended a meeting at which a current financial crisis was involved and a series of bitter decisions on expenditure was required of the assembled gathering of ministers in charge of spending departments, I fancy he would be surprised at the way in which the matter would be managed, and the conclusions which were almost invariably arrived at. There would seldom be a paper to discuss. Instead, the Prime Minister, with a face clouded like that of Jupiter Pluvius, would ask the Chancellor of the Exchequer to report on the serious financial situation, which had apparently burst on an astonished administration with the unpredictability of an earthquake if not actually of the Second Coming. Thirdly, whilst he would have expected a most careful analysis of the relative priorities he would find in the end that the only acceptable proposal to emerge would be the wholly irrational imposition of a fixed percentage cut all round, with only a few and very limited exceptions. When they got back to their departments, even experienced ministers would be quite surprised to find their permanent secretaries waiting to receive them with positive suggestions which had evidently been discussed within their departments and between departments without their previous knowledge.

I am myself a real believer in Cabinet government as essential to a democratic constitution. But I would immediately require to make a number of qualifications. In the first place, Cabinet Ministers have as I pointed out in a previous chapter a great deal too much to do and much more to do than ministers in other countries. Overwork is the mark of a bad system of administration or a bad administrator. Since I always managed to acquire a greater amount of leisure than my British colleagues, I do not believe the fault lay in myself.

I believe simply that our system of government is inefficient partly because it is overcentralized. Ministers should have plenty of time to think, and plenty of time to go about visiting their own outstations and comparing experience in this country with that abroad, and should spend far less of their time in the House of Commons dancing attendance on the division bells. I was a far more efficient Minister of Education in the House of Lords than in the House of Commons precisely because I was able to travel and was not bound to attend every night to vote in divisions which ought never to have taken place. I would have been infinitely more efficient than I was if either of the regions of England or those of Scotland and Northern Ireland and, to a lesser extent, Wales, had been free to develop their own systems subject to central inspection and some financial control, and if I had been given more freedom to examine standards and curriculum, and the general relationship between school, further, higher and vocational education and training.

The relationship between individual Cabinet Ministers and their colleagues, in particular the Chancellor of the Exchequer, is a matter of more or less conscious deception. So long as he remains in charge of a department a minister is not allowed to disclose how far the decisions for which he is responsible are personal decisions of his own or decisions of the Cabinet as a whole. Thus, one of the first decisions I was made to adopt as Minister of Education in 1957 was in favour of making the educational grant to the local authorities part of the general grant as recommended by the Chancellor rather than a matter of special grant as it had been hitherto. I had never fully understood the importance of the controversy, but on the advice I received from the department I fought it tigerishly from beginning to end. When it was obvious that I was beaten, I asked my advisers whether, in view of the defeat, I ought in honour to resign.

They seemed surprised at the question, assured me that it was not so, and supplied me with an excellent series of speeches to make in the country, where the agitation against the general grant system was apparently fashionable and deeply felt, explaining that it really did not matter much after all, and this, indeed, proved subsequently to be the case. In the meantime, whilst I was uttering these arguments, all the teachers' organizations and all the educational papers pilloried me as the person responsible for the change of policy and I had to remain discreetly silent, not merely as to the fact that I had actually opposed it, but even as to the fact that it was the policy of the Cabinet as a whole, inspired largely by a triple alliance of the Treasury, the Prime Minister, and the Ministry of Local Government. As I was relatively inexperienced at the time, I found all this very surprising and bore it with much tooth sucking and muttering. How much the preservation of this deliberate mystification of the public by conventional morality may be really essential to good government I am not now able to say. I now understand the reasoning behind it, but what seems to me to be particularly odd is the fact that everybody outside the government not merely accepts it, but is apparently really deceived.

As I was not, and am not now, a believer in the art of leaking, I did nothing to undeceive them, as I suppose many less simple-minded ministers would have done.

I would in fact have found my life as a minister easier had my relations with the Treasury been different. Among other duties, the Treasury has the necessary but unenviable task of seeking to control public expenditure. This it does by methods which are perhaps more suitable to the days of Gladstone than a modern Chancellor. On the whole, the Treasury commands the most gifted and capable civil servants. In the Treasury there is an official for each spending department who spends weeks and months discussing almost every item of expenditure with an opposite number in the spending department. Each item has to be separately justified. If, at the end of the year, it is for any reason not spent, it stands to be confiscated by the Treasury. If there is any over-spending, a separate supplementary estimate will require approval. My own feeling has always been that the system is over elaborate, effectively encourages spending up to the hilt, and interferes with department autonomy and ministerial responsibility. I have often wondered whether it would not be more economical to give a department a budget which it must not exceed and tell them to make their own economies in order to stay within it.

The strangest episode of the year is when, in deepest secrecy, the Cabinet meets to hear the Budget. It is far too late to do anything effective about it. On the only occasion that I can remember when a Cabinet showed signs of disapproval only a few cosmetic changes were possible. I quite understand the reasons for complete secrecy about details. The slightest breath of an indiscretion, let alone a deliberate leak, in the days or weeks before a Budget, would cause fortunes to be won or lost, more or less disreputably, in speculation. But why should the structure of taxation be subject to the same degree of secrecy? A new tax, or a new system of taxing ought to be discussed, like any other new form of legislation, years in advance of action, a long time before the rates at which it is to be levied or the date on which it is to be introduced are decided. What is needed is so much publicity in advance and so much discussion that the speculator will have all the tips he wants from the press and not have to rely on titbits of confidential information. The structure of taxation ought to go through Parliament at a different time, and after adequate discussion. The rates should continue to be a matter of secrecy, and the general strategy and tactics of the economy should be separate again.

XXXIII

THE ROAD TO ESCAPE

I return to my point of departure. We cannot go on as we are, for we are living in the City of Destruction. Even if our problems were purely economic, if we went on as we are we should need to go on borrowing indefinitely and this is manifestly impossible. The pound would sink lower and lower. Prices would rise higher and higher and wages and earnings would go on pushing them up. The unemployed would slowly increase in numbers, and in competition with our neighbours we would show poorer and poorer results. Sooner or later the creditors would foreclose. Sooner or later the crunch would come, either as the result of a slow slide or a sudden convulsion. We should then have to choose between a long and painful climb back to our old values which we would have lost in the crisis and a violent and sudden end to our old traditions, followed by a siege economy and a dictatorship of the right or left.

But, though the symptoms are largely economic, I do not myself believe that the underlying causes of our predicament are entirely concerned with economic policies. Even if our economic problems were solved by some change of policy or by a miraculous draught of North Sea oil, or by some other means, I do not believe that by such means alone we should be saved from shipwreck. The agony of Northern Ireland would still continue. Scottish and Welsh nationalism would still be with us. The unions would continue arrogant and oppressive, and their targets, the public, increasingly resentful. The alienation of the middle class would not abate. The remoteness of management from the shop-floor, and the workers' resentment against the centralized and faceless bureaucracies of the state, their employers, and their own unions would continue to break out in the form of more and more numerous strikes, official and unofficial. The growth in violent crime would continue, and moral standards would continue to decline. The problems of the

City of Destruction are not confined to wages, prices and unemployment. The processes of decay and disruption are far more deep-seated than that, and the symptoms will continue until the causes are removed. These causes are social and moral, political and constitutional, and not simply economic.

What is wanted is a clear-sighted vision of where we want to go and how we propose to get there. For my own part I offer a three-part prescription, a conscious return to the theory of limited government, a period of stability and legislative restraint, and constitutional reform. All three proposals are interrelated. Constitutional reform is a means of institutionalizing the theory of limited government and preserving the democratic process against elective dictatorship. A period of stability and legislative restraint in advance of constitutional reform is essential if we are to restore respect for law and digest the changes which we have made in recent years. The theory of limited government is the golden thread which will unite our policies into a coherent whole.

I am aware that this prescription will be attacked from three different angles. It will be condemned as reactionary by those who wish to see our society transformed into a people's republic or something excessively nasty to the right of Mr Powell. It will be criticized as excessively radical by those who think that there is in fact nothing fundamentally wrong with existing arrangements, or, perhaps more accurately, by those who think that there is nothing wrong which cannot be put right by a general election, a change of government or perhaps a coalition. Perhaps the most dangerous criticism of all may be that it is visionary, that even if we wanted to tackle the situation in this way, the chances of success are so small that even the attempt is fatuous.

I will answer this last criticism at once. My answer is that circumstances will compel us, are even now compelling us, to face the issues, that the issues are so interrelated that we shall be compelled to face them comprehensively so that our answers to each will depend to some extent on our answers to the others. Our unwritten and traditional constitution, at first sight so mysterious and even ramshackle, so asymmetrical in appearance, intellectually so difficult to justify, becomes on closer inspection, not indeed a nicely balanced mechanism like a watch, but an even better balanced organism like the human body or a hive of bees, or perhaps the molecular structure of a living cell. Each part affects the functioning of the whole, and, through the whole, the other living parts as well.

Why then not let it alone? It has served us well in peace and war. It has combined flexibility with inner strength. It has survived revolutions and social change, reformations of religion and civil wars. It has served tyrants and put them down. It has governed empires. Of human institutions only the Papacy surpasses it in continuity and prestige. Its pageantry, its tradition, its sheer adaptability, are natural possessions of immense, almost mystical, value. Why not let it alone? May not the same qualities which have seen it through so far preserve it yet again in the baffling changes of a revolutionary age?

Well, in a sense they may. For what I am suggesting does not involve doing away with the monarchy, a bicameral legislature, trial by jury, Magna Carta, an independent judiciary, representative government, or universal franchise. What I suggest is more democracy, not less of it. It is only the aberrations of recent years that need curbing, the tyranny of the organized minority, the heresy of party mandate and manifesto, the incontinent flood of legislation and expenditure, the increasingly unbalanced see-saw of party politics, the excessive centralization of bureaucracy in state and industry. The old constitution was limited and balanced. By giving more power to the people and taking some away from the party whips and jacks in office we shall be restoring and not destroying the balances and checks of our age-long institutions.

Well, is it impossible? My answer remains that while circumstances do not compel any particular answer to the questions or, necessarily, the order in which they should be faced, they will compel us to give an answer of some kind. Take the House of Lords for instance. It is clear that another Labour Government will attempt to abolish it or in some other way alter the status quo. I have given my reasons for saying that if the next government is Conservative it would be crazy not to enact a Conservative answer and so pre-empt the threat. The Labour plan would, in the end, amount to one-chamber government, and, in the absence of change in the voting system and some limitation on the powers of Parliament this amounts to elective dictatorship. We should have institutionalized centralized democracy and it would only be a matter of time before the substance of limited government was forgotten altogether.

By contrast, a Conservative alternative would move towards the institutionalizing of limited government, and, if I am right, an elective House is the only really satisfactory choice, since an elective House alone carries the necessary moral and political authority to challenge executive govern-ment. But this means both that the voting system must be prescribed and the size of the constituencies delineated. It is obvious that neither could be identical with those of the existing House of Commons; otherwise the result would be a mirror image of it. Even if elections were held at a different time, the result would be a mere clash between the two Houses. Thus, the size and shape of constituencies cannot be seen in isolation from the issues of devolution to Scotland, Northern Ireland, or Wales. Similarly the voting system cannot be seen in isolation from that obtaining in the European Parliament, or, if devolution becomes law in some form in isolation from that adopted in the devolved assemblies.

Or take the problem of devolution. This cannot be seen out of relation to the powers actual and theoretical, of the Westminster Parliament, and it is really stupid to believe that, unless we opt for a no-change policy, the issues raised by devolution to Scotland can be isolated from those concerned with Northern Ireland, Wales, or the rest of England. Nor can the various voting systems to be adopted be ignored or treated out of relation to all the others, the European and Westminster Parliaments, the elective second chamber (if there is one), the devolved assemblies, and the existing, or changed local authorities. The resulting questions can only be evaded in the short term if we opt for the status quo, and if, when we have done so, the problems of devolu-tion and Scottish, Welsh and Irish separatism disappear, which they are unlikely to do. None of these problems will simply go away. If one is to be tackled, all must be considered and solved.

My conclusion is, therefore, that the charge of being visionary or unpractical simply does not stick. It is my critics, not I, who have their heads in the clouds, or, more probably, planted firmly in the sand. My next discussion, therefore, will be concerned with ends and ways and means.

XXXIV

RETURN TO LIMITED GOVERNMENT

I return to the criticisms described in the last chapter. Am I being too radical or too reactionary, or am I being merely visionary, with my head in the clouds? I have answered 'no' to the last question, because the issues are there and cannot by any means be avoided. I will now discuss the others.

But am I being reactionary? In a sense, I am. My diagnosis is that the society we live in is in process of disintegration. This diagnosis does not differ profoundly from that of the extreme left, or the extreme right in politics. Extremists accept my diagnosis, but greet it with enthusiasm. What I fear, they welcome. They believe that our society is on the verge of perishing, but they wish it to do so. They believe it irredeemably corrupt and wish an alternative society to emerge. What this alternative society may be is not a matter of agreement even on the left. Most would agree to call it socialism. But between the socialism of Moscow and Peking, let alone the innumerable unrealized utopias pursued, say, in California or Thaxted, there is much to choose from, and, perhaps, little in common. Nevertheless, in their belief in the imminent destruction of existing society, and their desire for it to happen they are at least united. Inspired by Marx and his successors, they would say that what we are witnessing is the collapse of capitalism by virtue of its inherent contradictions, that, as feudalism gave way to capitalism, and, in its last phase, capitalism to imperialism, so socialism is being nurtured in the womb of capitalist society and will at length emerge, assisted no doubt by socialist midwives, not without trauma, but ultimately to the benefit of mankind.

There is not much fascism in Britain at present, but, for the first time since the war incipient fascist tendencies can be seen. The basic creed of fascism depends upon the intention to defeat socialism by the adoption of socialist methods, a centralized state based on a single party, a programme of reforms which would require dictatorial methods if it were to be effective or maintained in existence for any length of time and the exploitation of popular grievances by the substitution of alternative targets to the capitalist class. This is why they seek to make the most of racial or religious conflict or anti-semitism. Fascism is thus a means of defeating Satan by invoking Beelzebub.

Against all these I am for the slow climb back. But this means an end to the politics of envy and class war. The whole history of politics can be crystallized into a protracted war between freedom and authority. But whose authority, and within what limits should it be exercised? And what is freedom, freedom to do what, and, again, subject to what restraints?

For a time it was thought that the advent of democracy made the debate meaningless or at least superfluous. Instead the debate rages more furiously than ever. Owing to the way in which democracy came about, the battle between freedom and authority has been thought of in terms of a conflict between two different sets of people, the rulers and the ruled. At first the problem seemed to be to control the executive by Parliament, and later to control Parliament by a gradual extension of the franchise. Thus we lost sight of the real contest. Ought government to be unlimited in powers? Ought the general good to be the only criterion? Since the advent of democracy it has come to be seen more clearly that the real battle is within ourselves, or between one individual and another. Legitimately or otherwise, we all represent authority in one form or another, even if only as voters. More frequently we hold some form of authority ourselves, as Members of Parliament, as county councillors, as judges or magistrates, as landlords or employers, as Trade Union officials, or even as chairmen and secretaries of purely voluntary societies. And if we are all rulers, so also we are all part of the ruled, as householders, as motorists, as taxpayers, as subject to criminal and civil obligations, or even as husbands and wives. The law, which, in its nature, is concerned with compulsion, encroaches on our freedom at a hundred points each day.

So the battle is not over, and will never be over so long as men and women live together in communities. But I believe that, for the last hundred years or more, a false view has been taken of the nature of authority in a free society. I call this false theory legal positivism, because on the whole it corresponds to the view that it is in the nature of sovereignty to exercise unlimited powers of rule, powers of rule, that is, unlimited by any lawful qualification, and that the power of the ruler, by which, in a democracy, I mean the anonymous majority constituting the electorate, can legitimately be exercised solely in the interests of what some call the common good, although many still prefer the less philosophical phrase of the greatest happiness of the greatest number. I believe this theory to be unjust and productive of many of our present evils, in particular of class war, and what have been called the politics of envy.

In place of this doctrine, which I believe to be both cruel and false, I believe it is time to revert to an older political creed. I will call it the theory of limited government. This claims that there are limits to authority, however composed, beyond which no government may stray, limits which will never be observed unless they are policed either by judicial enforcement like those enshrined in the American Bill of Rights, or by political or institutional checks and balances like the division of power under the American constitution or, in years gone by, in our own between executive, judiciary, and legislature, or between the two Houses of Congress or Parliament, or between Washington and the States of the Union.

The theory of legal positivism has had a long predominance in the West. This has been largely due to two very simple facts. The first is that there are more and more people in the world and in any given country. So the more crowded we are, the more restraints become necessary, and the more organized we must become. The second is that it has been found in practice that human relationships all place social and economic power in special hands. Thus whole classes of people become vulnerable to misuse of this power in the hands of those who wield it, and so must appeal to the organs of the state for protection against the injustice which this involves.

But the time has come to assert what I believe to be the true political creed of the West. Legal positivism has never been part of the true Western tradition, Christian or pagan. It has never been the way in which legislators and judges have spoken, or the way in which ordinary people have thought and acted about their duty towards their neighbour. Despite the legal positivists, we continue to think and speak as if there were rights and duties which neither the authority of the state nor the common good which the state is supposed to promote may legitimately override. We think that there are rights of individuals and minorities of which they may not lawfully be deprived by a vote of the majority. In short we believe that the state, like other institutions, was made for man and not man for the state, and that what is true of the state is true of lesser communities, the family, the village or township, the corporation, the social class, the trade union. Each and all are entitled to their several loyalties. But each and all are subject to limits which they may not overstep.

This is no academic philosopher's dream. It is a policy for action, and it spells the end of the politics of envy, and class war. It speaks for the division of power, and therefore for freedom. It speaks against absolute authority in any form including that of Parliament. It speaks against permanent subordination, ugly forms of discrimination, penal taxation, confiscation. It is, in fact, the unspoken basis upon which the Universal Declaration of Human Rights, and its child, the European Convention, were based. It means that in future, though the mark of democracy may be universal suffrage, the test of its practice must be the extent to which the anonymous majority respects the rights of minorities and of individuals. It will achieve the decentralization of government power. It will favour the reduction of taxation, already recommended as a step towards stability. It is suspicious of bureaucracy. The return to limited government is thus one of the touchstones against which policy should be measured.

All this can be done with a change of direction only. But in the end the advocate of a return to limited government must face a dilemma. Is he to content himself with changes of policy which can be achieved for a time simply by executive action or refusal to act? Or ought he not rather to face the need for constitutional change? Theories of government which are not institutionalized are seldom lasting. Speaking for myself, I am not prepared to shirk the issue indefinitely. The theory of limited government must be built into our constitution as it is into the American. It does not suffice simply to assert it as a temporary expedient. It is something which is right for mankind and not simply a question of party policy. If this is right we must look forward to constitutional change.

XXXV

A PERIOD OF STABILITY

As a means of recovery, indeed as part of the return to limited government, I believe this country requires a period of stability. This involves a period of at least one whole Parliament of consciously legislative restraint amongst moderates of all parties. Change is good. A country without the means of change is not likely to preserve its traditions. This means that the best means of preserving continuity is actually to allow society to evolve continuously by making its ethos one of continuous and pragmatic reform. But in recent years, change has been too rapid, too rapid, that is, for the public mind to digest, or the need for continuity to accept. We need a period of recovery, of consolidation, a period in which men and women can take stock of the situation in which they find themselves, the road along which they have travelled, and the direction they wish to take during the next stage of their journey. For the last thirty years the atmosphere has been one of almost constant upheaval. If this had brought success in its train, I suppose that one could welcome it, as stimulating, exciting, even inspiring. No doubt some such prospect was envisaged at the time of the Queen's Coronation when, with premature optimism, people started talking of a new Elizabethan age. But the upheaval has been accompanied by almost constant failure, made more dispiriting by comparison with the almost equally constant successes of other nations operating within our own traditions of freedom under law and starting from a position less favourable than our own.

This constant innovation accompanied by as constant a decline would of itself demand a period of respite. But we have now to recognize that neither law nor political institutions, neither morals nor social habits can be respected if they are to be in a constant state of flux. Laws, like religion, were not made to be constantly reformed. Even the Chinese are beginning to realize that the doctrine of continuous revolution can be overstated. Men need some degree of security if they are to plan for the future, some measure of continuity, something certain to look forward to even if they are expected to work hard during the present. In the last thirty years we have gone too far and too fast, much further and much faster than is justified by the popular will of which our new elitists of the left have been only too contemptuous.

Whether we be of the right or of the left, the printing presses have got to stop. The ever increasing flow of decreasingly respected legislation, Acts of Parliament, Orders in Council, Statutory Instruments and Regulations must be brought to an end in exactly the same way the governments must be stopped printing those decreasingly valuable floods of paper money in the financial sphere. Let the resources of government and the Civil Service be devoted to clarification, consolidation, codification and repeal. Legislators must be taught that legislative incontinence is a crime against society, that every evil or injustice, real or imagined, should not necessarily breed a new law or an ingenious new restriction.

If, which is not now possible, it were left to me to devise an election programme, whether for the left or the right, I would promise reduced taxation and a clarification of our taxation laws. I would promise reduced public expenditure, certainly. But I would also promise to do as little as possible in the field of general legislation apart from constitutional change, no bold new schemes requiring government expenditure, no shake-ups in education or health provision, no more nationalization measures, no comprehensive schemes for new race relations, sex relations, or industrial relations, no new bodies brought into existence to remedy the irremediable. Let the people of Britain, I would say, take a breather for a change, concentrate on their economic problems and consider what should be the next steps in their constitutional development. Let them not be continually worried by new projects for reform. Let them catch up with what they have, and consider at their leisure where they wish to go.

Such a scheme is obviously an ideal one, and one would not be able to live up to it in every field. In particular, in constitutional law it would not be possible to avoid important change, or at least the creation of machinery to make change possible. But the minimum of change for the time being is, I believe, what the people need, and I rather suspect it is what the people want. For the time being they want no more upsets. They want stronger government, but much less of it, and above all, a minimum of new legislation. Let them be allowed to concentrate, for a change, on their own lives, and the economic problems of the country. Of ideologies, even my own should be given a rest for a while, except in so far as this is satisfied by a reduction in the level of taxation, and in the pace and intensity of change.

The programme I have suggested would have considerable practical consequences for the leadership of all parties. It would not, of course, affect any measures required by the financial or economic situation. The rubric there would be to accept any measures, however unpalatable, which could be expected to bring about immediate and lasting improvement. Nor would it affect our study of the various constitutional problems which I have sought in what I have written to bring to the surface. I would prefer these studies to be pursued at leisure. A delicately balanced organism like the British constitution ought not to be tampered with by amateurs at short notice. But, for reasons already given, I doubt whether the situation can be constrained to remain static sufficiently long to allow of such leisurely treatment, and, even if it can, we should need to set up new machinery for bringing about constitutional change and processing the various projects for doing so.

With these two important qualifications, a period of rest and recuperation is what I would prescribe for the British nation. Legislation designed to bring about radical and irreversible changes should be avoided. Socialists should eschew all further nationalizing, Conservative enthusiasts of various kinds would have to drop at least for the time being grandiose schemes for the 'couponizing' of education, or patent ideas for changing the whole face of housing and health policies. They would have to abandon all wideranging schemes for the reform of trade union law, although, no doubt, particular adjustments in all these fields might have to be undertaken in the light of events. The various pressure groups, whose object is to bring about sharp changes in morals, or social discipline, or crime and punish-ment would need to be resisted except in the case of over-whelming urgency.

In the field of doctrine, the period of respite should be used for a clear reconsideration of the path which we wish our nation to be treading. What are our moral values? What place do we allow to religious or spiritual experience? What part in the world do we wish Britain to play? What sort of democracy do we wish to practise? What is nation-hood, and what is our nation? Until we have a picture of the things we really believe in we shall go on blundering about in the City of Destruction, until one day we find that the kissing has to stop, either because we discover that our main policies spell only disaster or because disaster has overtaken us owing to the fact that they add up to absolutely nothing at all.

XXXVI

A NEW CONSTITUTION
FOR BRITAIN

I am sure that Britain needs a new constitution. I am sure that it should be of the 'written' or 'controlled' variety, and that it should therefore contain entrenched clauses if it is at all possible to bring this about. The object of such a constitution should be to institutionalize the theory of limited government. The method adopted should have the effect of giving more power to the people nationally and locally in order to prohibit their supposed representatives from passing unwanted legislation. So far as it is necessary to protect minorities or individuals against mob law or populist politics from the left or right, judicial remedies should be provided. But these are much the least important part of the whole package. The root of present evil lies not in an excess of democracy but in too little, too much power in parties, whips, officials, cabinets, and a House of Commons elected in the present manner for a period terminable by dissolution and possessed of all the powers of Parliament. In short too little power is given to the people.

These being the desired purposes, I do not wish to be dogmatic about any particular set of proposals. Changes should be undertaken after discussion, and we are still in the early stages. If, therefore, in what follows, I put forward my own positive suggestions it is not because I imagine that what comes out of discussion will resemble in any particular detail what I have sought to put forward. I put them forward in detail solely to illustrate the kind of thing I have in mind, and to show that I am not simply talking generalities devoid of constructive ideas.

We have in Britain no basic laws. Any law can be altered in a single session of Parliament by a bare majority in both Houses, or in two sessions by a bare majority in one. What we have to do is to pass Acts of Parliament creating a constitutional framework, and then to ensure that either as a matter of law or as a matter of practical politics it is difficult (though not impossible) to alter it in a reactionary direction, difficult in order to defeat the passing wishes of an ephemeral majority, not impossible because the object is to trust the people and confide in them more power and not less.

But we must begin with what we have, that is Royal Prerogative and Act of Parliament, and the first thing which these must do is to set up machinery for constitutional reform, not as the last Royal Commission with terms of reference so limited that the total perspective is lost sight of, nor with options so universal and vague that no conclusion can be foreseen. An ongoing body is required to map out the whole field, but it should be one to which Parliament could give instructions in one field after another as to the general line to be followed. Its task would then be to draft a Bill which would then be placed before Parliament in the ordinary way, and ratified by referendum. If passed by referendum it would then become law and could only be altered or repealed by analogous legislation, i.e. reference to the Commission, Act, and renewed referendum.

I visualize the Commission setting about its task by tackling problems *seriatim*. Some, such as the creation of a second chamber, may have become so urgent that they may have to be solved, at least provisionally, in advance of the Commission. The total product might take very many years. But, as each chapter was framed, I visualize it taking the form of a draft Bill for consideration by Parliament. When passed, the Bill, on becoming an Act, would be submitted for ratification by referendum, and, on being confirmed by referendum, would become alterable only by a comparable process.

This would make our constitution 'written' in the technical sense, since the power of Parliament to alter or amend it would, to that extent, be restrained. Only an Act confirmed by referendum would suffice to change it. The government of the day would, of course, retain the initiative to propose changes of this kind. If there were changes in the general law (as distinct from financial measures) they would have to pass both Houses, the second of which would have been elected on some system of proportional representation. If they involved constitutional change, a referendum would also be necessary. Obviously in the course of this procedure many possibilities would be discussed and some projects would be abandoned either as unnecessary, as too controversial, or as not sufficiently urgent. But the mechanism for change would be available, and when it yielded a positive result would be subject to popular control.

Although I visualize a limited constitution, I do not myself visualize a separate constitutional court. Questions of constitutional law of widely differing importance occur from time to time in ordinary legal proceedings at every level, and become subject to the ordinary hierarchical structure of appeal when they are of sufficient magnitude. This involves an extended role for the judges, but it is not a role which differs in principle from the functions they perform at present in criticizing the actions of the executive. Since the legislature will have made the law, it will take the form of statute, and it will be the function of the courts first to decide, as now, what the statute means, and then to apply that meaning to a concrete dispute, taking into account on the way any other legal rules. I visualize the whole body of English law as constantly evolving under a partnership between judiciary and Parliament, with Parliament in the superior role, but limited in powers, which, of course, could be extended or diminished by the ultimate sovereignty of the people. We should have retained our characteristic institutions, with their modern accretions deriving from our membership of the European Community and with the addition of regional organizations. But Queen and Cabinet, bicameral legislature, Common Law and Statute would continue to be the order of the day. Only the tendency to elective dictatorship would have been reversed, and a free nation, decentralized, democratic, would go on its way enjoying diversity in unity, so long as peace and order in the world at large allowed it to enjoy the spaciousness of freedom under the rule of law.

What would the finished product be like? In addition to Queen and Parliament organized in two Houses, there would be regional assemblies, Scotland, Northern Ireland, Wales, and the regions of England. Each functioning part would have legal limits, part imposing the human rights accepted by Britain internationally, and part defining the frontier between regional and central government. The central Parliament would have reserved powers in case of emergency and alone could promote legislation altering the basic laws to which the referendum procedure would apply.

The government would, as now, consist of a Cabinet and ministers composed in such a manner as to command a majority in the Lower House. This House, as now under government initiative, would have a monopoly of central finance.

The regions would be entitled to govern within the limits of the constitutional powers devolved on them, and the convention on human rights. For this purpose they would be entitled to some share in the national revenue, and increase the rate of certain taxes exacted nationally within their region. They would also be entitled to exact some taxes locally. They would have their own executive, and the method of election, unless otherwise decided, would be some system more or less conforming to single transferable votes. My hope would be that local authorities forming the lowest tier of government would cover areas smaller than those created in 1972. I regard regional government as primarily a devolution of power from the centre, but also, secondarily, as acquiring an accession of strength from some of the vast new single-purpose authorities and from the over-large local government units created by the 1972 legislation.

I do not conceal the fact that I would like to see some forum for discussion giving effect to my belief that the British Islands need some place in which matters of internal interest could be thrashed out. I realize that this is a long-term project and would probably not be seen in my lifetime. It would not seek to go back on the Irish Treaty or diminish the rights of the Channel Isles or the Isle of Man. It would be a Benelux type arrangement within the Common Market. The failure of the Sunningdale agreement, and the successful Protestant general strike which followed it were partly at least the result of a failure of a British dimension in all Irish affairs. The old United Kingdom of Great Britain and Ireland broke up because it did not recognize the profound desire of the native Irish for self-government. A federal structure might have served to preserve it. But the time for that is past and the opportunity missed.

Nonetheless, the problem of the British dimension still remains, and can only be solved by some ongoing forum of discussion within the European Community but on a confederal basis.

I do not believe that such an aim is either visionary or impracticable. Within the British Isles, our places of abode are virtually interchangeable. We have a common interest in the seas round our shores, shared incidentally by the Isle of Man and the Channel Isles which are not separately represented in the Westminster Parliament, and are increasingly impatient of the restraints imposed by Home Office control. We have common or shared problems of housing, unemployment and internal security. Our currencies are linked and virtually interchangeable. Our political philosophies and constitutions are broadly compatible. There is no language barrier between us. Our peoples are so cognate that it would be virtually impossible in these islands to find a single individual without some admixture of Celtic, Saxon, Norman or Viking blood. We already work together privately, and, as it were, by stealth, but will not easily acknowledge our co-operation in public. We are full of nit-picking criticisms of one another, but almost incredibly loath to admit our common traditions, or the manifold debts owed by each to the other. It is a lamentable piece of hypocrisy that the British and the Irish peoples cannot walk together in amity hand in hand, and in the interests of both countries. Until they do, I fear that, in Ulster at least, there will be recurrent bloodshed.

But all this is by the way. Apart from our Ulster troubles, this book is about British politics, and our relations with Ireland are, to my sorrow, part of foreign affairs. The way forward for Britain is by way of constitutional change, institutionalizing the rule of law, and making elective dictatorship impossible.

XXXVII

BRITAIN AND THE WORLD

Though this is not a book about foreign affairs, they have never been far from my mind. The affairs of the human race are evidently moving, at an increasing rate, towards some sort of climax. If not in sight, some sort of world order is a necessity, and, if it does not come about, some sort of world catastrophe is, I believe, inevitable. We have to ask ourselves whether in these days of destiny we are doing our duty towards the remainder of mankind.

Ever since it was said offensively, but with a certain degree of truth, that Britain had lost an empire, but failed to find a new role, I have been pondering the effect upon the rest of the world of the eclipse of Britain. The loss of our empire is nothing to do with the case. Given our exhaustion after the Second World War, the attitude of the two super powers towards us, and the development of nationalism in the so-called Third World, that was inevitable, though its effects have been unfortunate and unsettling for the rest of mankind. We left a void when we vacated our imperial role, and nothing adequate to fill it has been provided by those who were so anxious to see us go. What is more disturbing is our failure to play an honourable part in world affairs after our imperial role was over.

But we had a role before we had an empire. We did not become a great people because we had an empire. We won an empire because, after the Act of Union, we became a great people. We have lost sight of our destiny, because we have lost our independence and we have lost our independence, because since 1945 we have been content to borrow money, spend it on current consumption and not to pay it back. With loss of independence comes loss of self-respect. Without independence, there can be no foreign policy, and there can be no self-respect without financial independence. Our loss of independence has nothing to do with loss of empire. It has nothing to do with our membership of

NATO or the EEC or any of the other international organizations of which we are part. It is a direct result of our continued failure to put our own house in order, and the result has been the growth of selfishness, violence and permissiveness, separatist movements where the spark of nationalism is present, and, where it is not present, pressure groups, discontented minorities, and, on the part of all too many, the desire to impose unacceptable ideologies on the inarticulate mass of the people.

But Britain owes a duty to the world. The first part of this duty is to put our own house in order. It is no good prattling about world poverty and starvation, nor even of improving the lot of the less fortunate of our own community whilst we are taking more out of the pot than we are putting in. This continues to be the case so long as we continue to borrow without repaying and spending the proceeds on current consumption. To talk in terms of idealism while this remains true is nothing but hypocrisy in its crudest and original sense.

But we have a further duty to the world even when we have put our house in order. The great landmarks in human history come from comparatively few and comparatively small areas. Athens, Rome, and Jerusalem are three examples. Whoever else may wish to be added to this list, this small island has already contributed enough to be a fourth. A country that has trodden the road that leads to greatness may only abandon her high calling on pain of extinction. The failure of Britain to cope with the problems of a free society will mean much more than would be provided by the spectacle of just any middle-sized nation degenerating into a motley crew of snivelling mendicants. It would be treason to our past. It might even deal a mortal blow to the hope of mankind for a civilized future, based on evolutionary development, moral standards and freedom under the rule of law. When we see men groan under single-party tyranny and posturing rulers, each declaiming against the wider application of the things we cherish, one would have no qualms about the future if all that their oppressors were denouncing were the absence of Cabinet government, trial by jury, party politics, and the prerogative of dissolution. But what they are really doing, as everyone knows, is to find some excuse for throwing away the things which these institutions symbolize, some pretext for abandoning the constraints of civilized behaviour, either towards their own citizens or their near neighbours. What they are really doing is to point to our own failure as a means of justifying military rule, summary executions, one-party government, or religious or political persecution, in the worst cases aggressive war, and even genocide. The spectacle of an enfeebled Britain living on others without returning their assistance gives no encouragement to men to adopt principles which we once professed, but cannot now be seen any longer to practise successfully.

English has become the second language of the world. It is through our tongue, and the writings in it, that men have discovered ideas, have dreamed dreams, have grasped realities before but dimly apprehended. It is through the eyes of English-speaking men and women, and the magic of their translations from Greek and Hebrew which they have carried with them through all the continents that they have received and studied the only text-books of morals and politics – which rival the scriptures of communism as guides to map our way through the new and unknown age of technology. For us to fail, for us to betray their trust, would be more than failure. It would be the ultimate treason.

So Britain has a duty to the world. She has also specific duties to Europe, of which she is part, the Commonwealth, old and new, of which, in different ways, she is the parent, to the United States of America, now so immensely more powerful than ourselves. This, as I have said, is not the place to elaborate foreign policies.

But we have these duties. There are men and women all over the world who stand for the same things as we, and these things are threatened, both by those who believe in nothing, and by those who believe too confidently too much. If we fall, who, in the end, will stand? Others may be richer. Others are certainly more powerful. But, if we fall, I am convinced that we may well carry Western civilization down with us in our ruin. Therefore, I say with Milton:

Let not England, or rather Britain, forget her precedence of teaching nations how to live.

INDEX